D0269765

FAITH FOR LIFE

FAITH FOR LIFE

by

John Ashplant

**SELECTED TELEVISION TALKS BROADCAST BY
REV. JOHN ASHPLANT ON WESTWARD TELEVISION**

First Edition 1979

© Westward Television/John Ashplant 1979

All rights reserved by the publishers
Arthur James Limited of Evesham, Worcs., England.

Ashplant, John Douglas
Faith for life.
1. Christian life
I. Title
249   BV4501.2
ISBN 0-85305-215-8

No part of this book may be reproduced in any form
whatsoever without written permission from the
publishers except in cases of brief quotations used in
written reviews and critical essays printed in
newspapers and magazines.

Gibbons Barford Print, Wolverhampton

FOREWORD

Westward Television have transmitted live late night epilogues under the generic title of *Faith for Life* almost since the Company began broadcasting in 1961. The programmes, which have had a wide range of subject matter, have been extremely popular.

In addition to providing a main contribution to the *Faith for Life* series, the Reverend John Ashplant has also been Westward Television's Free Church Religious Adviser providing helpful advice and guidance for the rest of our religious programming output, all this in addition to his ministerial responsibilities in Somerset.

For those of you who enjoy *Faith for Life* I hope that this book will bring back pleasant memories and added comfort on special occasions, and for those of you who live outside the Westward Television region, I hope that these messages, best read perhaps at the end of the day, will bring pleasure and comfort into your lives.

Ronald Perry,
Managing Director,
Westward Television,
Plymouth
July, 1979

CONTENTS

WHATEVER HAPPENED TO YESTERDAY?

WHATEVER happened to yesterday? And the day before? And all the other days before yesterday?

One answer I have heard given is — into the limbo of the past.

Odd word "limbo". It comes from the Latin "limbus" which means 'border, hem, edge'. I suppose that is where our word "limb" comes from. The other meaning of "limbo" is "a place of neglected and forgotten things".

Is that what happened to yesterday — neglected and forgotten? No! because what we are today is very much the sum total of all our yesterdays.

What is your attitude to the past? Are there things in it that have the power to hurt you? My experience of countless confidences entrusted to me as a minister convinces me that a great many people are still brooding over past mistakes and failures.

Let me tell you about a plum tree! There it was in an old orchard, lying in ruins on the ground. It was Autumn and the ripe Victoria plums were still there, but the whole tree had crashed. What had brought it down — the heavy crop, the stormy winds, old age? No! It had been ravaged by insects which had attacked it over a long period. The owner of the orchard was asked, "What are you going to do now?" Back came the answer in a flash: "Gather the fruit and burn the tree"

That is exactly what to do with the past — gather the fruit and burn the incident. Of course the past has much to teach us. The man who says he has no regrets is either a fool or a liar. The wise gain rich fruits of understanding and insight from the past, perhaps most of all from those experiences they bitterly regret. "Gather the fruit and burn the tree."

Some people keep harping on their past sins, almost as though they enjoy recalling them. Do you know what the Bible says about past sins? That God has put them "behind His back, never to be remembered again". There's a wonderful thing! Then why do we go behind God's back and dig up old sins that God buried long ago? If God can forgive, who are we to refuse to accept forgiveness?

Take regrets. How often have I heard sentences begun with "If only — I had done better at school ... got a better job ... done this and not that ... said this and not that ..."

And take resentments about past injuries. If you hurt someone, do all you can to put it right and burn the tree. If someone has hurt you, forgive and burn the tree. Resentment is a poison that can embitter your entire being being even to the point of making you physically ill. And often the cause of the resentment is too trivial for words. Talk about making mountains out of molehills!

Do you know what happened to Gilbert and Sullivan whose music has brought such enjoyment to so many? You would think that they must have had the happiest and jolliest of relationships. But in fact they never spoke to one another for years. And do you know why? They bought a theatre, and Sullivan bought a carpet for it and Gilbert thought he had paid too much for it. They had a row about it and at one point took each other to Court! They never spoke to one another again! Gilbert would write the words and send them to Sullivan, and Sullivan would write the music and send it to Gilbert! And if ever they had to take a bow on the stage, they would stand at opposite ends of the stage and bow outwards so as not to face each other!

What I am asking you to do is to make sure that the past has no power to hurt you. If there is something you must put right, put it right. If you are nursing a grievance, nurse it no longer. If you have not accepted God's forgiveness, accept it now and be at peace. "Gather the fruit and burn the tree."

It is my belief that the past, the present and the future are in the hands of God.

A HEALED WOUND

DO YOU know about pearls?

Some people make the mistake of thinking pearls go with pleasure. In a way they do. Women wear them at dinners and dances and on other notable social occasions.

But pearls have to do with pain and suffering.

Do you know how this beautiful marine gem comes into being? It is made by the oyster. It begins when a small insect or parasite punctures the shell of the oyster, often at the point where the two shells meet. And through the hole there enters an alien body, it may be a grain of sand or a bit of grit. This acts as an irritant and causes the oyster great pain. At this point all the resources of this little creature are directed to the point of pain, and a very precious secretion is exuded to close the breach made by the parasite and save the life of the oyster. The result is a pearl.

The pearl is born in pain. It is the symbol of stress. It is a healed wound.

In the last book of the Bible, Revelation, there is a magnificent picture of the Holy City. Twelve gates lead into the city from all points of the compass, and St John says that "every gate is a pearl". The way into heaven is the way of the pearl. I suppose that is why we sing "open up them pearly gates"! But the pearl stands for pain and suffering — is this the way to heaven?

The problem of suffering is the biggest single obstacle in the way of faith. Why disease germs? Why malformed babies? Why natural disasters such as earthquakes and hurricanes? Why suffering at all? Couldn't God have managed things differently?

Let's look at one aspect of suffering for a moment — where nobody suffers, nobody cares. It was the death of a young mother of heart failure that prompted Sir James Mackenzie to study cardiology. It was Aberfan that led to the Coal Board's decision to remove potentially dangerous slag heaps near coal mines. Lighthouses are built by drowned sailors. Roads are widened by mangled motorists.

Everybody suffers sooner or later. You may think that some suffer more than others, but it comes to all of us at one time or another.

Some people use suffering as a means of learning the mind of Christ. It was the blind Milton who wrote "Paradise Lost", the deaf Beethoven who composed the incomparable Ninth Symphony, the imprisoned Bunyan who gave the world "Pilgrim's Progress". Their pain became pearls.

Jesus Christ chose to take the hard way, the Way of the Cross, to suffer for the sins of the world.

The pearl in the oyster is made in darkness. It grows to perfection in darkness. When brought out into the light it possesses all the colours that ever were. The death of the oyster brings about a lovely and beautiful thing.

That is why we say that Jesus Christ is the Pearl of Great Price.

DID THE DEVIL DIE OF THE COLD?

THERE IS a village in Devon where, so it is said, the devil died of the cold! Would you know where to find it? Well, it is the village of Northlew. If you draw a line from Okehampton to Hatherleigh, Northlew is just north of that line. And it was there, so they say in those parts, that the devil died of the cold. Mind you, Northlew is a pretty bleak spot in the Winter.

Not far from Millbay Dock in Plymouth you will see a signpost to Devil's Point. Devil's Point is at the entrance to Plymouth Harbour, where Devon and Cornwall are separated by a narrow strip of water. But why "Devil's Point"? Because the water at this point is a whirlpool of dangerous currents — devilish, in fact. From the shore it looks peaceful enough, but I have it on the authority of one who nearly drowned there that "devilish" is the word.

Do you believe in the devil?

Of course, none of us believes in the sort of devil pictured by medieval artists, complete with horns and tail and toasting-fork! But I do believe in the existence of an evil force which can, and often does, make havoc of our lives.

In the East, there is a strong belief in the existence of such an evil force or spirit. For instance, a person's name is of very great importance and is rarely said aloud because it is thought that lurking evil spirits, once they know the person's name, will have the power to hurt him!

Billy Bray, the Cornish miner and preacher, certainly believed in the existence of the devil. In one of his incomparable sermons, Billy described one of his many encounters with "that ould tempter, that ould vagabond".

"Friends," said Billy, "last week I was a-diggin' up me taturs. It was a wisht poor yield, sure 'nough; there was 'ardly a sound one in the whole lot. An' while I was a-diggin', the devil come up to me and 'ee says: 'Billy, you think your 'eavenly Father do love 'ee, do 'ee?' 'I reckon 'ee do,' I said. 'Well I don't', said ould tempter in a minute, 'and I tell 'ee what for; if your 'eavenly Father loved you, Billy Bray, 'ee'd give you a perty yield of taturs; so much as ever you do want, and ever so many of 'em, and every one as big as yer fist, for it bent no trouble for your 'eavenly Father to do anything!'"

This was almost too much for Billy. But he recovered his balance just in time and recited a catalogue of all the good things the Lord had done for him since his conversion: how He had given him a clean heart, a soul full of joy and a home to go to when he died. And this was definitely too much for the devil!

"Bless 'ee, my dear friends," said Billy, 'ee went off in a minute, like as if 'ee'd bin shot — I wish 'ee 'ad — and 'ee didn't 'ave the manners to say 'Good Mornin'!"

Three times, so we are told, was Jesus tempted of the devil in the wilderness — "If you are the Son of God, change these stones into bread ... the world is yours if you will obey me ... if you are the Son of God, throw yourself off the pinnacle of the Temple and let's see whether your Father will save you".

Jesus's reply was, "Get thee behind me, Satan".

So — where does the truth lie — did the devil die of the cold at Northlew? Or is he lurking in the treacherous waters off Devil's Point?

When next you are making out your expense account, or sending in your tax returns, or making a decision, take a quick look over your shoulder — you might just see the devil standing there!

If you do — tell him to go to hell!

DOES IT MATTER WHERE?

WHAT IS it that takes us into a cathedral or abbey or some other great church building?

The answer is quite simple: deep down inside ourselves we know there is more to life than this physical and material world. At least we hope there is.

One of the most visited places of worship in England is Buckfast Abbey, just off the A38 near Buckfastleigh, about halfway between Exeter and Plymouth, on the edge of the National Forest of Dartmoor. The Abbey is a poem in stone, the depository of devotion and skill and craftsmanship. The original Buckfast Abbey was founded before the 10th Century, but the present cruciform church was built by the monks themselves between 1907 and 1938. The Benedictine monks who live here believe that work is one of the great disciplines of life and is meant to be offered to God.

Perhaps, like me, you have visited the Abbey more than once, never without capturing something of the peace of God that rests upon this place of worship.

But I recall something else that made a deep impression on my mind when I first visited Buckfast Abbey. As you leave the Abbey grounds, you come face to face with a little Methodist chapel just across the road from the Abbey's main gates, and you are struck at once by the contrast between the two buildings — the Abbey, a magnificent building, a thing of infinite beauty; the little chapel, like so many other Nonconformist places of worship, simple, unadorned, severely functional. And as you go inside the chapel the theme of simplicity continues — the central pulpit, the simple communion table, the modest organ. You stay long enough to note how spick and span the little chapel is — clearly, somebody loves it very much.

When this happened to me, I found myself asking the wrong question — was the one better than the other? You see, both great Abbey and little chapel are houses of God, places of worship. Both are precious in the eyes of God. Both are loved and cherished by the people who worship there. Both are spiritual homes for human beings haunted by the Spirit of God.

I spent an hour with the Abbot of Buckfast. What a gracious man of God he is. He showed me things visitors do not normally see. He asked me to stay for a meal, and he said something to me I think will interest the members of the little chapel. "You know", he said, "the Methodists were here before the monks returned." This I recalled was indeed the case, for the Methodist chapel was opened in 1881, whereas the monks returned from France in 1882. And then he told me how very much the monks enjoyed listening to the Methodists singing their hymns.

Does it matter where we worship God? Whether it be a great cathedral church or a tiny wayside chapel? I think not.

Jacob, one of the Bible's most colourful characters, was running away from God. At the end of the day, exhausted, he fell asleep with a stone for a pillow. He dreamed a dream and in it he saw a ladder set up from earth to heaven, with angels going up and coming down. When he woke up, he said, "surely the Lord is in this place and I knew it not." He called the place where it happened Bethel, which means "House of God".

The writer of the last Book of the Bible, John of Patmos, was in a concentration camp when he wrote the Book of Revelation, a prisoner in chains. Do you know what he said? "I was in the Spirit on the Lord's Day."

Great Abbey or little chapel, it does not matter.

What does matter is that you should acknowledge your

HE NEVER STOOD ON HIS DIGNITY

THE WORD *Dignity* has been coursing through my mind lately. What is dignity?

Often we associate dignity with position and power. We think of occasions of pomp and circumstance — the State Opening of Parliament when the Monarch and the Lords of the Land wear their robes and regalia, the enthronement of a Bishop, the making of a Mayor or Lord Mayor, or the more frequent spectacle of the procession of clergy and choir into church at the beginning of a service. Such occasions, we say, are occasions of great dignity, as indeed they are.

But dignity is not something you put on. Real dignity is quite different, though I am sure that the wearing of the symbols of office and responsibility help to create within the mind of the wearer a sense of privilege and responsibility — I know this for myself, for when I put on my preaching gown, I am reminded of the importance of what I am about to do.

We talk about another kind of dignity — human dignity. We say that every human being has a dignity of his own because he was made in the image of God and shares the life of God. If you read Psalm 8 you will see the big question is, "What is man?" Is he just another animal? Does he count for anything? Is he simply a tiny, insignificant speck on the face of the earth? The answer given by the Psalm is that God made man "a little lower than the angels".

That is why the senseless slaughter of human beings in war and the dying of millions by starvation is such a sin — they deny human dignity.

We talk about the the dignity of old age. We picture some very old person who has grown old gracefully and whose face bears the unmistakable marks of serenity. Serenity and dignity — are they, then, two names for the same thing?

As always, I want you to look with me at the one person in whom we find true dignity — Jesus Christ.

He did not occupy a position of power and importance. You would not have found Him in a procession of the mighty. He never stood on His dignity. He never demanded that people should show Him respect. And yet they instinctively did.

If you want to know what dignity is all about, look at Jesus. Note His composure. He was subjected to all kinds of mental and physical torture, but He remained composed throughout it all. His own disciples argued the toss about who should be the greatest in the Kingdom of God, but instead of becoming angry with them, He quietly and patiently talked to them about the real Kingdom.

Note His compassion. He was always concerned about people in their need. Not a single opportunity to help someone was allowed to pass.

Note His humility. When He came into Jerusalem on the first Palm Sunday along what is now called Palm Sunday Road, He came riding upon a donkey. Not in regal splendour, not with pomp and circumstance, not with any show of self-importance. Jesus was born humbly. He lived humbly.

Note His purity. He was a good man. None better. Even His enemies could find no wrong in Him, though they tried hard enough! He once talked about the pure in heart. Well, He was the purest of the pure in heart.

Composure, compassion, humility, purity — this is what dignity is made of. And so, when He came to His trial before Pilate, and when He suffered all the indignities that could be heaped upon Him, He remained silent. In the whole of the Passion story there is nothing more impressive than the silence of Jesus.

Dignity is a deep inner strength born of knowing God. Dignity is the calm assurance that all things are in God's hands. Dignity is the mark of the pure in heart, for they have seen God.

WONDERFULLY UNCONCERNED

THE ANCIENT borough of Shaftesbury is set on a hill in Dorset. A pleasant market town, with the added attraction of being recommended by the medical profession as a health resort. Time was when Shaftesbury — Shaston, to give it its earlier name — was a holy place. Its great Abbey, in which lay the bones of King Edward the Martyr, was a place of pilgrimage, many believing that the bones themselves worked miracles.

It was at Shaftesbury that King Canute died — the gentleman who fought a losing battle with the tide — though he was not buried at Shaftesbury, but at Winchester.

All this in the tenth and eleventh centuries. By the 18th century things had changed for the worse. Shaftesbury became a collection of vagrants, gypsies, prostitutes, thieves, fortune-tellers and smugglers, all herded together in tumble-down shacks at the foot of Gold Hill. The narrow streets were unsafe at night, many an unfortunate traveller being set upon by highwaymen.

Smuggling was common. Even the church was not entirely exempt, for beneath the vaults of St Peter's church more than one cask of forbidden brandy lay hidden. Taverns abounded everywhere and drunkenness was rife. Religion was at a low ebb and Shaftesbury was in need of a spiritual awakening.

As always, God had a man for the hour, a certain John Haime, a boy of humble parentage who grew up to become a soldier in the Queen's Regiment of Dragoons. While serving in the Dragoons he heard Charles Wesley preach, and it was this that led to his conversion. He became a close friend of John Wesley, and it was partly because of this friendship that John Wesley visited Shaftesbury in 1750, and preached there at a spot described by him as "the most riotous part of the town, where four ways met."

When Wesley had done preaching, a constable came up to him and said "Sir, the Mayor discharges you from preaching in this borough any more."

To which Wesley replied, "While King George gives me leave to preach, I shall not ask leave of the Mayor of Shaftesbury!" When Wesley came to the town to open a new Methodist Chapel in 1766, he made this entry in his "Journal": "I went to cold, uncomfortable Shaftesbury and spoke exceeding strong words."

We thank God for men like John Haime and John Wesley. We admire the way they stood their ground and risked martyrdom for the sake of the Gospel.

Now, more than 200 years later, Christians can attend their places of worship without let or hindrance, and with the Mayor's blessing! We are persecuted no longer.

Is that why some of us have grown so spineless and flabby and indifferent? Times have indeed changed, but man's needs remain the same. True, we have coined more respectable names for vagrancy and prostitution and theft, but man remains essentially what he was two hundred, two thousand years ago — a sinner in need of salvation.

Reflect on this single horrific fact: Since the year 1900, we human beings have killed (not let die) one hundred million of our own kind; and God knows how many fellow-human beings we have let die.

Shaftesbury's need two hundred years ago was a religious revival. And what Shaftesbury needed then, the whole world needs today. When John Wesley returned to Shaftesbury five years after the opening of the town's first Methodist Chapel, this is what he wrote in his "Journal": "Came to Shaftesbury and preached to a numerous

GIVE IT TO THE JUMBLE SALE!

HAVE YOU been to any good Jumble Sales lately?

Judging by the number advertised in the local papers, it would seem to be the most popular money-raising gimmick in the Charity business. If a Youth Club or a Women's Meeting needs to raise cash in a hurry, up goes the cry "Let's have a Jumble Sale!"

And what a rush there is when the doors are finally opened! People queue for anything up to a couple of hours, and the first ten minutes is sheer murder — everybody grabbing the best buys — winter coats for 50p, pairs of shoes for 10p, an old wireless set for 25p (in good working order!), a pram for 50p, assorted woollens and frocks and skirts going for a song, men's clothing, books, pictures, and an endless assortment of odds and ends. Within twenty minutes the main attack is over and only a few skirmishes remain before the cash is counted and the mopping-up operation begins!

Was it worth it? Well, judging by the way in which Jumble Sales multiply, the answer would seem to be a resounding "Yes".

I must say I am sorry that the Jumble Sale has pushed that colourful character, the Rag-and-Bone Man, off our streets. "Rags and Bones" is a cry seldom heard today for the simple reason that people have given "it" to the Jumble Sale.

There is another colourful character, whom I have mentioned before, who would have something to say about the use of the Jumble Sale for the raising of money for Church funds. In fact, I reckon he turns in his grave at Baldhu Church, Cornwall, every time a church holds a

Jumble Sale. I am referring, of course, to Billy Bray. Billy held to the view that only "the best" should be given to the Lord.

At one time, when attending a Missionary Meeting, Billy was visibly vexed to hear that money had been raised by the sale of "rags and bones". When he got up to address the meeting, he said: "I don't think it is right, supporting the Lord's work with old rags and bones. The Lord deserves the best, and ought to have the best."

And when Dr Spurgeon, the famous Baptist preacher, heard of this, his comment was, "Well done Billy! This is good and sound divinity".

Now I am not advocating the abolition of Jumble Sales as I believe they perform a useful function. There can be no doubt, however, that Billy Bray's contention that "the Lord deserves the best, and ought to have the best" is sound divinity. To Billy, the whole of life belonged to God, thus everything was an offering to God.

What a wonderful thing it would be if only we put this principle into practice! It would change our whole attitude to life.

If only we came to see that an honest day's work is an offering to God, that when a man digs a lump of coal out of the earth he is handling something sacred, that the whole of life in all its aspects is meant to be an offering to God, a God who deserves and ought to have the best.

This same idea lies behind worship, which, literally, means worth-ship — something that is worthy of being offered to God. This same instinct lies behind the presenting of invaluable art treasures to the Church for the beautifying of its buildings and the enhancing of its worship.

Billy Bray was right. God deserves the best, and ought to have the best — don't you agree?

A CHANGE OF HEART

ONE of the loveliest stories I know was written by Oscar Wilde. It is called "The Selfish Giant". Let me tell it in my own words.

Every afternoon the children used to come and play in the Giant's garden. It was a beautiful garden with soft green grass. Here and there, among the grass, were the most beautiful flowers looking like the stars of heaven. In the garden were twelve peach trees which in the Spring came out in delicate blossoms of pink and pearl, and in the Autumn were laden with luscious fruit. The children loved to play in the Giant's garden.

He was away at the time, visiting his friend, the Cornish Ogre, but after staying with him for seven years, ran out of things to say and so he returned to his castle.

When he saw the children playing in his garden, the Giant was very angry. "Get out of my garden," he shouted, "this is my garden, not yours"! The children ran for their lives, falling over each other with fear. The Giant built a high wall all round his garden and put up a large notice which read: "Trespassers will be prosecuted". He was very a selfish Giant.

The children had nowhere to play. They would wander round the high walls of the Giant's garden and talk about the good times they used to enjoy inside.

When Spring came again, a remarkable thing happened. All over the country the trees came to life again, and the flowers bloomed brightly everywhere except in the garden of the selfish Giant. There it was still Winter, with snow and ice on the ground, and not a flower in sight. The Giant could not understand it. Why had not

Spring come to his garden as it had done to everybody else's? But it had not, and neither did Summer, and Autumn brought no fruit. And the birds that once sang so beautifully in the Giant's garden never came near it.

One morning the Giant was awakened with the sound of the most lovely music. The Spring has come at last, he thought. Looking out of his window he saw a wonderful sight. The children had crept back into his garden through a hole in the wall. In every tree there was a child, except one, and the whole garden was ablaze with colour. But in one corner of the garden it was still Winter, and there, under one of the peach trees, was a little boy too small to climb into its branches.

The giant's selfish heart was softened by the sight, and, moving quietly out into the garden, he picked up the little lad in his huge hands and gently lifted him into the tree. The little lad put his arms as far as he could round the Giant's neck, and kissed him!

Well, to cut a long story short, the Giant knocked down the high wall, took away the forbidding notice and allowed the children to play in his garden every day.

But one thing saddened the Giant's changed heart — the little lad he had helped into the tree was not seen again. Day after day, the Giant would ask the other children, "Have you seen my little friend?" And always the answer was "No."

The Giant grew old and feeble. All the folk round about said he was not long for this world.

It was Winter. Not that the Giant minded any more because he knew that Winter was merely the Spring asleep. One morning he looked out of his window and saw something very wonderful. Though it was Winter, there, in one corner of his garden it was Spring. The peach tree there was covered with pink and pearl blossom, and there, standing under the tree was the little lad he had helped into its branches long ago.

Somehow the old Giant managed to get out into the

garden. When he came near to the little lad, he noticed that in his hands were the prints of nails.

"Who dared to hurt you?" cried the Giant angrily. "Tell me and I will kill him!"

"No," said the little lad, "these are the wounds of love."

The old Giant knelt at the little lad's feet and said, "Who are you?"

The little lad smiled and said, "Once you let me play in your garden. Today you are coming with me to my garden, which is called Paradise".

When the children came to play in the garden that afternoon they found the Giant lying dead under the tree, and his body was covered with blossom.

A PILE OF DEAD LEAVES

DARTMOOR abounds in folklore. Ask any of the moorland folk and they will tell you that some exceedingly odd things happen in the remote hamlets of England's Last Wilderness. Only recently, I was asked to exorcise a ghost that was troubling a family at Wotter.

All the stories I have come across have a common theme — the eternal battle between Good and Evil, and in all of them there is an attempt to explain natural events in terms of the supernatural. The devil figures largely in these stories, as do the pixies, the former being entirely evil and the latter entirely good and kind, especially to children.

There is the story of what happened at the Inn at Poundsgate on October 21st, 1638. A stranger came in from the fierce storm and ordered a pot of ale. As he drank, the landlord's wife noticed a cloven hoof beneath the man's cloak, whereupon she presumed they were entertaining the devil himself. The stranger drained his tankard, threw some money on the counter, and disappeared into the storm. The landlord's wife picked up the coins and put them into a basin. When next she looked into the basin, the coins were gone and in their place was a pile of dead leaves.

Later the same day, a thunderbolt struck the church at Widecombe-in-the-Moor, a fine old building erected at the beginning of the 16th century following the revival of tin mining. When the church was struck that day, four people were killed and sixty-two were injured, and because this happened only a few miles from the Inn at Poundsgate, the people of Widecombe were quite certain that this was the work of the devil. Today we would call it an "Act of God" — they called it an "Act of the Devil"!

One thing is certain; the inhabitants of Dartmoor believed in God. All that was good and true and noble was attributed to "The One Above", and all that was wicked was ascribed to the devil. Obviously, this is too simple an explanation of life, but it does express an intuitive belief in a world beyond our own, a spiritual world.

There are many ways by which people become convinced about religion. Intuition is one of them. There are some things we know without being told. We did not learn them at school. We did not read them in a book. We just *know* them.

We know that —

> LOVE is better than HATE
> KINDNESS is better than CRUELTY
> BEAUTY is better than UGLINESS
> TRUTH is better than LIES
> GOODNESS is better than BADNESS

How do we know? We just know! Call it insight, call it intuition, call it what you will — the important thing is, it's there and you know it.

If you have seen the film "Sound of Music" you must have been deeply moved by the story on which the film is based. But tell me this: What was it that made you want the Von Trapp family to escape from the Nazis at the end of the film? Something inside you said "they *must* get away." What was it? Some would call it humanity. I call it *GOD*.

There is something in us that responds to sacrifice and selflessness. Who can be unmoved by the story of the Russian Nun, Elizabeth Pilenko, who, on Good Friday, 1945, saw an hysterical girl in the queue for the gas chamber at Ravensbruck Concentration Camp, and said "Don't be frightened. Look, I'll take your turn" — and went to death in the girl's place, on Good Friday?

Deep down inside you there is this intuitive belief in

LADY DAY

I ASKED a boy of six earlier this week, "What's special about next Sunday?" He screwed up his face and replied, "I'll have to look up my diary".

What on earth could a six-year-old have in his diary — I didn't even know six-year-old children kept diaries! I was intrigued, to say the least. Back he came: "There's nothing in my diary about next Sunday." So I told him that next Sunday would be Mothering Sunday. "That's funny", he said, "My diary says that March 25th is Lady Day!"

Mothering Sunday has an interesing history. Originally it was the day when servant girls were allowed to go home to their mothers. Now it is the day when Mum gets some tangible expression of the family's gratitude for all she does for them, day in and day out. It is the day when we say, "Three cheers for Mum!" And then almost in the same breath we say "Carry on, Mum... we'll do it again next year!"

There was a very close relationship between Jesus and His Mother. When He was born, and the Manger-Crib was visited by the shepherds, and later by the Wise Men, we are told that "Mary kept all these things and pondered them in her heart." You can imagine the loving care that Mary lavished upon her Son in those early weeks and months and years. Like every other mother she must have had her moments of anxiety, if not panic. There was the time when she and Joseph took Jesus to Jerusalem for the Passover Feast for the first time. Jesus was twelve years old, and on the return journey they lost Him. You can imagine how frightened she was. And when they found

Him, in the Temple, He said something that she pondered even more: "Didn't you know that I must be about my Father's business?"

According to a very strong tradition, Jesus and His Mother shared the grief of bereavement, for it is believed that Joseph died when Jesus was in his teens, leaving Him as breadwinner for the family

Mary knew what it was to lose a son, in two senses. First, when Jesus left home to become a travelling preacher, and later when they murdered Him on the Cross. And she was with Him when He died — such is the love of a mother.

I think of a little old woman who for years visited her son in a mental hospital three times a week. There was nothing they could do for him. He was a pitiful sight and it broke her heart every time she went. But she kept going right to the day he died, often hardly knowing how to drag one foot after the other.

So, on Mothering Sunday, by tradition a happy day, when children present their mothers with posies in Church, let us spare a thought and a prayer for the not so fortunate — the mothers of Asia nursing their starving children, their little bodies twisted into grotesque inhuman shapes by the sin of the world, the mothers of the children who have died, a familiar voice silenced, never to be heard again — no one can plumb the depths of such heartache as this — ageing mothers nursing their fond memories of two generations ago; and let's not forget those women who would give almost anything to bear children of their own, but who cannot. One of the strange ironies of life is that while many children are born unwanted, some who want them dearly cannot have them.

At the Service of Infant Baptism, the minister says to the congregation, "This child belongs to God."

Let us see to it that all our children are given the chance to get to know Mary's Son — Jesus Christ.

GOD AND STRADIVARI

ANTONIO STRADIVARI was born about 1644, in the Italian town of Cremona. At first he worked for Nicholas Amati who was a maker of violins. Both invented improvements to the instruments and earned Cremona the title "The Town of the Violins".

Soon Stradivari branched out on his own and began to make the violins for which he has become famous. He had a passion for turning a block of wood into an exquisite voice. He took endless pains with the varnish that turned them gold and red, inlaid them with ebony and ivory from his own designs, and lavished decorations on their cases.

He was a tall, thin man, ever wearing a white leather apron, and always at work. He lived frugally all his life for he had eleven children to bring up. For sixty years he dedicated his talents to the making of the most beautiful violins, and to this day he remains supreme in his craft.

Stradivari had no difficulty in selling his violins to the grandees of Italy, but he had no success in England. As a matter of fact he sent a collection to be sold in London at £4 each and they were returned as unsaleable! Recently, one of his violins fetched £84,000! The agent who bought this near-perfect example of Stradivari's work was asked what it was that made this instrument so much better than any other? He said he thought it might be the varnish that Stradivari made from a secret formula.

But surely there must be more to it than that! Do you know what Stradivari himself said? "God could not make Stradivari's violins without Stradivari!" Do you think that sounds pompous and egoistic? I don't. To me it expresses a truth of the highest importance — that men and women are at their best when they work with God, when the human and the divine are so intermixed that you can scarcely tell one from the other.

All the best work in the field of Art has been done by those who knew themselves to be handling the things of God. When you watch a real craftsman at work, the thing that impresses you is the reverence he has for the things with which he works. He is handling the things of God.

"God could not make Stradivari's violins without Stradivari." It is equally true to say that Stradivari could not have made his violins without God!

Where do we find the perfect example of the co-existence of the human and the divine? Yes, you are quite right — in the Person of Jesus Christ. In Him we see what human nature is meant to be. He is the only real man we have ever known. Those who lived with Him and worked with Him were in no doubt about His humanity. He worked with wood in the carpenter's shop at Nazareth. Just as Stradivari made violins with all the skill that God had given him, so Jesus made yokes for oxen with all the skill His Heavenly Father had given Him.

But Jesus is something Stradivari was not — the perfect union of the human and the divine. In the whole of history it had never happened before, and it will not happen again. Jesus Christ is unique.

There is a lovely little story told in the Bible with a rare economy of words. A merchant was looking for fine pearls when he found one of very special value. So he sold everthing he had and bought it: The Pearl of Great Price.

I cannot offer you a Stradivari violin! But I can and do offer the Pearl of Great Price, none other than Jesus Himself.

With Jesus there is nothing you could not do, no mountain you could not climb, no joy you could not know.

WHO IS THIS?

WHEN JESUS CHRIST entered Jerusalem on the first Palm Sunday, people turned and stared at the strange figure riding on a donkey and asked, "Who is this?" Jerusalem asked the question then, the whole world has asked it ever since. Hardly anybody doubts the existence of a man called Jesus Christ, but what so many find impossible to believe is that this man was at one and the same time both God and man.

Let's look at the evidence.

First, note the claim that Jesus made for Himself — He claimed to be God, He put Himself at the heart of His own message. No other religious leader has ever done this. What others have said is — "we are nothing; the truth is everything."

But listen to Jesus: "Come unto Me and I will give you rest... I am the Way, I am the Truth, I am the Life... before Abraham was, I am".

What are we to say to this? One of two things: either it is the claim of an incredibly arrogant and self-centred maniac, or it is true.

But think of something else: Jesus Christ lived a sinless life. As a matter of fact, the word "sinless" is not the word I really want — it's too negative and does not do justice to the wonderful life Jesus lived — but you get the point I am making. Those who observed Him closely said, "He did no sin." His enemies did their best to find some flaw in His character. They turned the fierce light of their hatred and hostility on everything He said and did. Not even they could find any fault in Him. Even Pilate had to admit, "I find no fault in this man."

Now this is a remarkable fact. When you read the lives of the saints like St Augustine, Thomas à Kempis, St Teresa, you find that without exception they are continually confessing their sins. But you never find Jesus confessing sin for the simple reason that He had none to confess.

And think of this. Jesus appealed to all sorts and conditions of men. His spell has fallen upon every century and every race. Nobody else has accomplished this. Aristotle did not — he was too Greek and too academic. Buddha did not — he was too Eastern.

Look at the disciples of Jesus, a motley collection of men indeed! Peter the big fisherman with the country accent, impulsive, impetuous. Compare Peter with the quiet, reflective, spiritually-minded John. And yet Jesus appealed to both. Compare Matthew the Jewish tax-collector with Luke the Gentile doctor — poles apart in many respects. Yet Jesus brought them together. You can go right through the twelve disciples and make similar comments. Somehow, this mysterious person Jesus Christ welded them into a force that was to turn the world upside-down.

It is the same today. In Westward Television's 'Talking Point' series, I have interviewed two students from Nigeria, a young man from Rhodesia, a girl from a London secretarial college, a professional footballer, a probation officer, a well-known naturalist, a youth leader, a business man — they all believe in Jesus Christ as the Lord of Life.

The appeal of Jesus Christ is universal — pop singers, university dons, actors and actresses, manual workers, office workers, rich and poor, high and low, men and women in every walk of life confess Him as Lord and Saviour.

How can anybody explain this phenomenon except on the ground that Jesus *is* different, that He is both God and

Man at one and the same time in a way we shall never be able to understand.

This is where faith takes over from reason, and it is faith the world needs so desperately today.

My own personal testimony is quite simple: In Jesus Christ I find a man big enough for every human situation, and a God who heals, restores, forgives.

BETWEEN GOOD FRIDAY AND EASTER DAY

THERE WAS a strange question that haunted the imagination of the Early Church: Where was Jesus between the Crucifixion and the Resurrection?

What was the Sprit of Jesus doing when His body lay in the tomb? In those silent hours between Good Friday and Easter Day, when heaven and earth seemed hushed and in suspense, where was Jesus? What was He doing then?

Here, it was felt, was a fascinating and dramatic theme for reverent enquiry. The Apostles Creed says He was "crucified, dead, and buried; He descended into Hell", and by 'Hell' the Creed means "Hades, the world of spirits."

We have a clue, if only a slight one, in I Peter, chapter 3, verse 19: "He went and preached unto the spirits in prison."

A book written at the same time as the New Testament, "The Gospel of Nicodemus", has a strange tale to tell of how on the day of Calvary, the underworld was lit by a strange unearthly light. Suddenly the voice of John the Baptist was heard proclaiming that Christ was on His way, whereupon Satan and the King of the Dead held a hurried consultation, only to be interrupted by a sound like thunder and a voice crying through the dark, "Lift up your heads, o ye gates, and be ye lift up, ye everlasting doors, and the King of Glory shall come in."

Satan and his satellites trembled as they heard the cry.

"Who is this King of Glory?" they asked.

And the whole domain of darkness shook as the reply came back, "The Lord of hosts, He is the King of Glory."

So into the realm of ancient night came Christ the

Victor from the Cross. Satan was bound, the King of the Dead dethroned, and the spirits in prison set free.

You may think that this is pure speculation, but I am not so sure. If Peter was right when he said that Christ went and preached unto the spirits in prison, then here is a message for all of us to hear, for we too inhabit prisons of one sort or another, some of our own making, others not.

Of two such prisons, one is the pressure of the world. The world of things is so much with us that it can easily become a prison in which the soul rots to death. There are people who tell me they have no time for religion because they have no time. They are totally immersed in and often obsessed by the things of this world. But Jesus came to set the prisoner free. What we need today is not a new dialectic or philosophy of material things — we need a Saviour with a key.

The second prison in which many incarcerate ourselves is the fear of death. We don't talk much about death today. It is the modern taboo. In Victorian times, the great taboo was sex; in our day we talk about sex until we are sickened by it. But we do not talk much about death.

Could it be that we are afraid of death? I do not mean that people are afraid of physical death, for when the time comes it is very rare for a man to be found afraid to die. No, the fear of death is something different — it is the fear that it is the end of everything, that there is nothing beyond.

Jesus has the key. It is called *Resurrection.* "I am alive for evermore."

If you are "a spirit in prison", my message for you is that Christ has the key that will set you free.

THE KISS OF LIFE

A CRICKETER nearly died after having been struck by the ball in the match between Glamorgan and Warwickshire at Cardiff. He was Roger Davis, a former pupil of Blundell's School, Tiverton, who was struck when fielding in what cricketers call "suicide corner" — just a few feet from the bat on the leg side. The bowler has only to drop one a bit short, and the fielder in this position is in grave danger. Davis was struck on the jaw and was knocked unconscious. As he lay on the ground without showing any sign of life, a doctor dashed from the members' enclosure and gave him the kiss of life. After fifteen long minutes, Roger Davis regained consciousnes and was rushed to hospital. Later the doctor said, "I was really worried because there was no sign of life."

It would appear that for a few moments, Roger Davis was dead, and was brought back to life with the kiss of life.

Do you recall the story of how God made man? You will find it in the early chapters of the Book of Genesis. It is said that when God had made man's body "He breathed into his nostrils the breath of life and man became a living soul."

You could call that the first kiss of life! So man was made in the image of God, the very breath that he breathes being given to Him by God Himself.

Do you recall the story of the risen Christ's appearance to the disciples on the first Easter Day? They were thoroughly miserable. The dreams they had cherished had died with Jesus on the Cross. All that they had hoped for — a new world, a new way of life, a new reason for living, had gone.

Then, wonder of wonders, the one they had seen die on the Cross appeared to them in the much loved Upper Room in Jerusalem. First he showed them His hands, His side, His feet, that they might know for certain that it was their Lord. Then, we are told, "He breathed upon them and said Receive ye the Holy Ghost."

What Jesus did then had the effect of breathing new life into them. Before He came into the room they were as good as dead. Now they were alive again.

Six weeks later came the first Whitsuntide. All this time Jesus had visited and re-visited them, putting the truth of His Resurrection beyond all doubt. And on the first Whit-Sunday, a comparative handful of Christians (one hundred and twenty) were together in one place when suddenly it was as if the place where they were was filled with the sound of a rushing mighty wind.

Whatever it was that happened that day they were utterly convinced that not only was the Living Christ with them, He was within them as well, and that He had breathed into their spirits His own all-powerful Spirit in whose strength they would be able to achieve the impossible. This Kiss of Life sent the Christian Church on its crusading way until it was to encircle the world, and indeed eternity.

Many years have passed since the Day of Pentecost. The world has got bigger and man has got cleverer. But neither has outlived the need for the Pentecostal experience.

The message of Whitsun is very simple: there are things we cannot do in our own strength, but there is nothing we cannot do in the strength and the power of God's Holy Spirit.

Most of us are too proud to admit defeat. We like to think ourselves capable of coping with all that comes our way. In our hearts we know we cannot. In our hearts we know we need God.

Let God breathe His power into your life. Let Him give you the Kiss of Life!

THE STRANGELY WARMED HEART

TWO HUNDRED and forty years ago a Church of England clergyman woke at five in the morning and began to read his Bible. After breakfast he read it again, again at the words "Thou art not far from the Kingdom of God."

That afternoon he went by invitation to St Paul's Cathedral where he heard the choir sing the anthem, "Out of the deep have I called unto Thee: Lord, hear my voice!"

He was in trouble and his problems were spiritual. Clergyman though he was, he lacked a living faith, and he knew it.

That same evening, he went, very unwillingly, to a society meeting in Aldersgate Street, London, where someone was reading Martin Luther's preface to the Letter to the Romans. This is how the clergyman described what followed: "At about a quarter before nine, while he was describing the change which God works in the heart through faith in Christ, I felt my heart strangely warmed. I felt I did trust in Christ, in Christ alone for salvation; and an assurance was given me that He had taken away my sins, even mine, and saved me from the law of sin and death."

The clergyman was *John Wesley.*

The date, May 24th 1738, is one of the most important in our national history, for what happened that day undoubtedly saved England from a revolution similar to that which was ravaging France, and indeed made an unparalleled contribution to the religious life of the entire world.

For the rest of his life John Wesley travelled the United

Kingdom, mostly on horseback, preaching the Gospel with such fire and conviction that thousands were brought to a new awareness of the relevance of religion. Bishop after Bishop refused John Wesley permission to preach in his diocese, thus forcing the evangelist to preach in the open-air and in such houses and meeting-places as were open to him. Often he had to contend with organised mob violence, more than once missing death by the skin of his teeth.

He made many visits to the South West, travelling from Bristol to Taunton, then on to Exeter and Plymouth, stopping long enough in the smaller towns and villages to preach the Gospel, no matter what the time of day happened to be. At Plymouth he would cross the Tamar into Cornwall where the people grew to love him after an unpromising beginning. When Wesley first moved into hostile Cornwall the odds against his even staying alive were not very healthy, as this entry in his "Journal" makes plain: "I was going to Crowan on Tuesday night when two of our brothers met me. They desired me for God's sake not to go up, for if I did, they said, there would surely be murder."

And yet when he paid his last visit to Cornwall in 1789, he passed through the towns and villages in a triumphant march, the windows crowded with people anxious to get a sight of him and give him their affectionate blessings.

Without wishing it, John Wesley and his followers found themselves separated from the Church of England. In the circumstances it was inevitable that another Church or denomination should be formed, and so it was that the Methodist Church came into being.

All over the country Methodist Societies were formed. Soon the movement was to spread to other parts of the world, not least to America. Today, the Methodist Church is probably the largest Protestant Church in the world with a membership of about forty million people.

Why was John Wesley called a Methodist? Simply

because his life was seen to be so methodical. He would rise very early in the morning to have time to read the Bible and pray. His whole life was efficiently organised down to the last detail. And as he ordered his own life, so he expected others to do the same.

What did John Wesley's Methodism stand for?

It stood for the Bible as the Word of God. Not that Wesley's approach to the Bible was uncritical — far from it. But he believed that the Bible contained the living Word of God by which men were meant to live. It stood for a belief in the need to change human nature. God had not intended that evil should mar human life. And Wesley preached Christ as Saviour. It stood for the belief that only by changing individual men and women would society be changed.

But it was on the foundation of his own experience on May 24th, 1738, that John Wesley based his preaching.

He knew the joy of sins forgiven!

He knew that his heart had been "strangely warmed"!

An assurance had been given to him!

And what had been given to him was available for all!

WAS JESUS EVER HERE?

"AND DID those feet in ancient time, walk upon England's mountains green? And was the Holy Lamb of God on England's pleasant pastures seen?"

William Blake thought it well within the bounds of possibility. One of the many unanswered questions about Jesus Christ is, what happened to Him between the age of twelve and the age of thirty? At twelve He went to Jerusalem with His parents to the Passover Feast, after which nothing is heard of Him until He begins His public ministry at about the age of thirty.

The West Country is full of legends that begin with the assumption that Jesus did come to England. If you go to Place Manor in Cornwall, the Curator there will tell you that Jesus came to that part of Cornwall, with his uncle, Joseph of Arimathea. Joseph was a merchant, and it is said that he brought the young Jesus with him on one of his journeys to England.

Nowhere is this legend more persistent than at Glastonbury in Somerset. Indeed, the area round Glastonbury is choc-a-bloc with legend — King Arthur, Camelot, and of course the legend of the staff that budded. It is said that when Joseph of Arimathea came to Glastonbury he thrust his walking stick into the ground and it budded. There, so legend tells us, the first Christian Church was built in England.

So it may well be that when next you see Glastonbury Tor as you travel through that lovely part of the West country, you will be looking at a spot sacred to the heart of God, and therefore sacred to all Christians. Well, was the Holy Lamb of God on England's pleasant pastures seen? Did He visit the West Country? Did He really come to Place Manor and Glastonbury?

I think it possible. To be honest, I want to believe it! But to be honest again, I have to say that it really does not matter one way or the other. What does matter is that we should know that the Spirit of Jesus Christ is present with us today in every part of the world, whether we realise it or not.

There is a lovely story told in the Bible about the woman who brought a box of precious ointment to the house of Simon the Leper in Bethany where Jesus was being entertained. That woman had good reason to love Jesus; He had given her a new lease of life.

To show her love for Him she took the precious ointment, worth a lot of money, and anointed the feet of Jesus with it. Judas Iscariot, with his eye on the money that the sale of the ointment might have brought into his own hands, said "What a waste!" You will recall that Jesus put Judas well and truly in his place!

The part of the story I want to bring out is this: It is said that when the vase containing the ointment was broken open, the fragrance of the perfume "filled the whole house."

When Jesus lived in Palestine His presence was confined to one place at one time. Even if He did come to England He did not stay long. The moment came when He had to go home to Galilee. But when Jesus died on the Cross and rose from the dead the fragrance of His presence filled the whole world. Set free from the limitations of the body, His Spirit pervaded the whole world from that day to this.

An old Scottish woman was asked: "How do you know that Jesus Christ is alive?" Back came the answer: "Because I spent an hour with Him this morning!" There are many people I know who would gladly testify to the reality of the Living Christ in their own lives. They talk with Him every day. They say that the Man who died on a cross two hundred years ago is alive today and can be found in any part of the world at any time. They will tell you that Jesus Christ is in England's green and pleasant land now. You think such people a little odd? I do not. In a world so obsessed with material things, somebody's got to have visions!

17

THE DONKEY IS NOT AN ASS!

EVERYONE has heard of Clovelly, that uniquely beautiful and picturesque fishing village in North Devon, visited by tens of thousands of people from all over the world every year.

Clovelly nestles in the wooded cliffs of the dangerous North Devon coastline, three miles from Hartland Point, fourteen miles from Bude. The village rises steeply from the shingle beach, zig-zagging its way to the top by means of cobbled streets lined on either side by some of the neatest and best kept cottages in Britain. Some of the cottages at the bottom end of the village are perched so close to the cliff-edge that one wonders how on earth they stay where they are.

Making your way down the cobbled High Street to the lower reaches of the village is a fairly easy task, provided you are wearing the right sort of footwear. But the return journey is a real test of strength. Will you ever get to the top? And won't you feel it tomorrow!

On the way up you may turn into the tiny Chapel-at-Ease of St Peter's for physical as well as spiritual refreshment. Higher up still, you may drop in at the Methodist Chapel and rest awhile. But the top is still a good way off, and even the younger ones who raced on ahead are beginning to feel the strain! But you arrive and it was worth it.

Think of Clovelly and you think of donkeys, working donkeys that plod their slow but sure way up and down the High Street, laden with foodstuffs, coal, suit-cases — in fact anything that can be carted from one part of the village to another is donkey work at Clovelly. What a pity the donkey is being superceded by the petrol engine!

On Palm Sunday each year (and I hope this is still the custom), one of Clovelly's donkeys has its greatest moment when it takes part in the Palm Sunday procession to the Parish Church of All Saints, to remind the worshippers that another of its kind had borne a divine burden into Jerusalem nineteen hundred years ago.

The donkey is not the ass it is often made out to be! I recall watching one being loaded at the bottom of Clovelly High Street. It would not budge. Why not? Because the load was not properly balanced and the wise beast of burden was not going to move an inch until matters had been put right! The art of donkey-loading lies in distributing the load equally on the animal's flanks. The donkey has the sense to know that a balanced burden is a lightened burden.

You and I do well to heed the wisdom of this oft-disparaged beast of burden. You must have noticed that when you are carrying suit-cases, two burdens are better than one. And this happens to be perfectly true in life as a whole, for if you have a burden of your own, a sure way of lightening it is by helping someone else to carry his load. Two burdens are better than one!

St Paul said two things which at first sight appear to contradict each other: "Every man must bear his own burden" and "Bear ye one another's burdens."

But both are true. Each of us has to bear his own burden in the sense that we have to accept responsibility for ourselves and for our actions. There are decisions and choices you alone can make. This is *your* burden and you must bear it. It is a part of the price we pay for being personalities.

But it is true also that we must bear one another's burdens, for this is the law of Christ. To give an example: the affluent Western nations must help bear the burden of hunger and want borne by the poverty-stricken peoples of the East. It is a plain Christian duty so to do.

A man saw a little girl giving a pick-a-back to a boy much bigger than herself. "That's a big burden you've got there" the man called out. Came the reply: "That's not a burden Mister, it's my brother."

18

ARE YOU SUPERSTITIOUS?

FOR SOME, the very mention of Friday the Thirteenth strikes terror into their hearts. It is odd that the number 13 should be regarded as unlucky, for in early Christian times the Jews looked upon 13 as definitely lucky. In our Western culture, from the time of Pythagoras (6th century BC), odd numbers have been considered more luck-bearing than even numbers.

How, then, did 13 come to be thought unlucky?

Numerous attempts have been made to explain it, the most likely of which has to do with the Last Supper when Judas Iscariot, the thirteenth guest, went out to betray Jesus. And why is Friday regarded as a day of ill-luck? The most likely explanation is that it was on a Friday that Jesus Christ was crucified. Yes, but the death of Christ was later seen to be the best thing that ever happened, so much so that Martin Luther called it "Good Friday", but try and tell the superstitious that there is nothing foreboding about Friday the Thirteenth and they will have none of it.

There are streets with no No. 13, airlines that will not have a seat number 13 on their planes, and there are people who go out of their way to make sure that they never sit thirteen at a table for a meal!

Superstition is widespread. Have you "touched wood" lately? Would you be prepared to walk under a ladder? Do you wear a lucky charm?

Let's look more closely at the three superstitions I have mentioned.

"Touch wood" probably derives from the Bible. In Old Testament times, when a man was on the run, if he managed to reach the wooden altar and touch it, he was reckoned to be safe — he was "in sanctuary".

The business of not walking under a ladder: Of course, you may be well advised not to if there is a man up there with a pot of paint in his hand! On the other hand, if you decide to walk round the ladder, you may get knocked down by a passing car! But what is the origin of this superstition? Again, probably religious, it being thought that the wall, the ladder and the ground together form a triangle, thus representing the Holy Trinity, God the Father, God the Son and God the Holy Spirit. It was therefore believed that the ground immediately beneath the ladder was holy and ought not to be walked on. Far-fetched? Yes indeed!

The carrying of a lucky charm may well go back to the dawn of history when man, believing there was something or someone outside of himself, carried relics of the god he worshipped.

I could go on for a long time about the origins of superstitious beliefs; it is a very fascinating subject. Of one thing I am certain: most superstitions have a religious derivation. Superstition is religion gone bad. It is a substitute for the real thing.

And this is what interests me. Here we are, living in the Age of Rationalism, when everything must be capable of being tested scientifically. Religion is rejected by the vast majority because it is incapable of being "proved" in the scientific sense. And yet this is the age of mascots, lucky charms, horoscopes, fortune-telling and superstition.

But you cannot have Christianity and superstition — they are poles apart. I prefer to believe that life is not in the capricious hands of something we call fate or chance. I believe that God made us for Himself and that in every life there is a God-given purpose.

Perhaps a word from the Bible is a good end-piece: "Regard not them that have familiar spirits, neither seek after wizards to be defiled by them. I Am the Lord your God. Trust in Me."

19

THE HEART OF THINGS

HOW WOULD you like to spend your annual holiday in a monastery?

Apparently, an increasing number of people are doing just that and feeling worlds better for it. Reports are coming in from all over the country of monasteries being asked more and more if there is accommodation for "transients". In some instances monks are building additional rooms to cater for the crowds who wish to spend a few days, a week, a fortnight or longer away from the day-to-day pressures. I am told that businessmen are high on the list of those who want to live the monastic life for a while, because, as they themselves admit, their lives are basically dishonest — not intentionally, but that is the way it works out.

They are worried by pressures, the pressures that say "Compete, get what you can, be ambitious, look after yourself." And the price of success is often more than they really want to pay. So they turn to the monastic life, not as an escape, but in an attempt to find the heart of things.

Young people too are finding their way to monasteries for a moral and spiritual pick-me-up. Not that they would wish to live "inside" all of the time, but after a few months "outside" they are ready to take time off to think through the meaning of life.

Those who go to monasteries as guests are allowed to do very much as they please — walk in the grounds which are invariably very beautiful, wander through the acres of farmland undisturbed, and generally give their souls a chance to catch up with their bodies.

The one rule they have to observe at certain times, including meals, is Silence. Real noticeable silence, not merely the absence of noise but a real, positive, creative silence. In most monasteries these days, the monks are allowed to speak, but only, as one monk put it to me, "when we have something to say. We never just chat or gossip."

At the end of the day, after Compline, in some monasteries there is what is called the Grand Silence. Just after eight o'clock in the evening, the men and women guests separate (married couples as well) and go their different ways. From then until the next morning they are expected to observe the rule of silence.

This then is a modern phenomenon — busy people, worried people, tired people looking for — and finding — a way to recover a spiritual dimension to their lives. You could say that such people are anxious to discover the heart of things, to find out what life is all about.

Well, what is the heart of things? In the Sermon on the Mount, Jesus says: "Do not store up for yourselves treasure on earth, where it grows rusty and moth-eaten, and thieves break in to steal it. Store up for yourselves treasure in heaven, where there is no moth and no rust to spoil it, no thieves to break in and steal. *For where your treasure is, there will your heart be also.*"

So your heart is in the thing that means most to you, the thing that you want more than anything else in the world. And what Jesus is saying is: some things last only for a short time, they are perishable. But there are other things that last for ever, they are imperishable.

More than anything else, you are a spiritual being. Of course, living in a material and physical world as we do, we need material and physical things. Jesus is not saying that the way to a full life is a total renunciation of the material world — that is an impossibility. But He is saying — take time off to find the true meaning of life, to obtain a spiritual awareness of your true self, to arrive at the heart of things.

Scientists now know that there are perhaps millions of other suns in addition to our own, and their conclusion is that it would be impertinent to assume that no life exists outside our own universe.

There is certainly another world outside our own space-time existence from which God is sending us spiritual messages all of the time. The only danger lies in turning a deaf ear to what He has to say!

Those people who spend their annual leave in a monastery are at least giving God a chance to get through to them. They are at the heart of things.

20

WHAT SORT OF MAN WAS JESUS CHRIST?

IT IS quite extraordinary how many people fail to think of Jesus Christ as a *man*. It can be only because they have not read the Gospel story with their eyes open.

Somehow the idea has got about that Jesus was a somewhat effeminate creature who went about Palestine wearing something that looked like a night shirt, someone whose life and message are more suited to women and little children than to men.

But just consider the facts!

He was a carpenter. It is more than likely that Joseph died when Jesus was a teenager. Incidentally, how often do we think of Jesus as a teenager? A baby cradled in a manger, yes, a man going about doing good, yes, but never a teenager! And yet there was a time when Jesus, the Son of God, was a perfectly normal teenager with a man-sized problem — the family breadwinner was dead, which meant that Jesus, the teenager, had to take on the job of keeping His Mother and the rest of the family.

Now, how do you see a carpenter? A weak, mealy-mouthed, effeminate apology of a man? Of course you don't! Like me, your picture of a carpenter is that of a real man with a strong arm and a straight eye.

He was a man of the open-air. When He left His home at Nazareth to do the work His Heavenly Father had sent Him to do, He had no permanent address, no generous expense account that enabled Him to live in the best hotels. In point of fact He spent almost all His time in the open-air. More than once He spent a whole night out in the open, at prayer. He walked miles, tramping from village to village, telling people about the Kingdom of

God. He knew the Galilean hills like the back of His own hand.

He commanded the loyalty and allegiance of other men. Fishermen mostly, men who admired manliness in another man, and who would not have been seen dead with a weak-kneed, mealy-mouthed, half-man. They knew a man when they saw one, and they had no doubts about the manhood of the one they came to call "Master".

He was the sort of man who could get angry. There was a day when He found the Temple at Jerusalem being abused and misused, turned into "a den of robbers" was how He put it, whereupon He promptly turned over the merchants' tables and sent them packing with a sting in their tails!

He was the sort of man who kept to His course. Even when the odds were stacked against Him. Even when the Temple authorities ganged up against Him and successfully plotted His death. His disciples, big fishermen Peter and the rest, ran for their lives. Not Jesus! He stayed and faced the music. He stood by all that He had said and done.

What a man!

I recall a "Harvest of the Sea" Service at the Plymouth Central Hall. The Hall was packed from floor to ceiling. The Polperro Fishermen's Choir sang a simple Gospel song entitled "I'll stand by until the morning".

I was reminded of the story of an old sea captain who has a medal which is probably unique. One night his ship received a signal from another ship in distress. He altered course and presently closed in on the battered hulk of the distressed ship which was wallowing in great seas and helpless because of its crippled steering-gear. Hour after hour he stood by, giving what help he could, until the storm died down and temporary repairs were possible.

Many days overdue, the crippled ship limped into San Francisco. When the people of Sydney heard of it, they sent the man a medal. On one side was his name, and on the other side these words: "The man that did stand by."

Jesus is that sort of man. He stands by in the storms of life, keeps close to us on the voyage, and sees us safely into port.

21

MANY KINDS OF HEALING

MARAZION, in Cornwall, three miles from Penzance, has a great attraction for me. Perhaps it is the name, which is a mixture of Aramaic (the language spoken by Jesus) and Hebrew. Just what the word "Marazion" means is difficult to say for certain. I suppose it means something like "The Lord's City."

It was at Marazion that that famous clergyman, Rev. Francis Henry Lyte, began his ministry as a curate. Opposite the Parish Church is the War Memorial which has on it in gold some lines from Lyte's most famous hymn "Abide with me".

Marazion is dominated by Mount's Bay which in turn is dominated by St Michael's Mount, the ancestral home of Lord St Leven. It is thought that the whole of this area was at one time a forest. Legend has it that Cormoran, the one-eyed giant, built the Mount in the middle of what was then a forest. Cormoran did not have a very good reputation with the people thereabouts — he is said to have raided the Marazion area many times to steal cattle. His wife was buried under Chapel Rock, having been slain by another giant. Later this forest was submerged to form what we now know as Mount's Bay.

In the 11th century Edward the Confessor founded a Priory on the Mount which became an important place of pilgrimage. It is said that the monks, on their way to the Priory, would sometimes wait on Chapel Rock for the tide to go down to make it possible for them to walk across the Bay on the causeway.

Chapel Rock has always fascinated me. For one thing, it is made of greenstone whereas all the surrounding rock is granite. Up to the 17th century there was a chapel on the Rock. Doubtless, the monks did use Chapel Rock as a stopping off place on their way to the Mount, but the people of Marazion assure me that it was used also for another purpose — for a resting-place for the sick as they were being carried on stretchers to the Mount for healing.

The ministry of healing has been neglected by most churches for too long. There are many clergymen and laymen who practise the ministry of healing with remarkable success. Healing is too big and too important a subject to be dealt with briefly. Even so, let me say one or two things about healing which I have found to be true:

Worship can be a means of healing. One of the members of my own church had a particularly troublous life. In the human sense everything went wrong. She was subjected to great stress and strain from sources beyond her control. Before she died she told me that whenever she came to church it was as if the Spirit of God cleansed her whole being and gave her peace. She said that the experience was beyond description. Of course she had to return to her everyday life, but she went back a new person.

Prayer can be a means of healing. Prayer is coming into the presence of Jesus Christ, the greatest Healer of all time. Some people wrongly suppose that prayer is a torrent of words. That is not what prayer is meant to be. When you pray for others, you should picture Jesus in your own mind and then deliberately bring the people you are praying for into the presence of Jesus and leave them there — He will do the rest.

Forgiveness can be a means of healing. If only we practised that part of the Lord's Prayer which says "Forgive us our sins, for we too forgive all who have done us wrong." This means Confession, something we Protestants do not talk about enough, and with true Confession will come healing and wholeness.

Healing does not necessarily mean the healing of the

22

IT ISN'T FAIR

I WANT to say something about the Christian attitude to Injustice.

"It isn't fair!" How often we hear this cry! And often it is true.

This man is unemployed through no fault of his own — a shipyard or car factory has folded up and with it has gone his job. Another man, with no better qualifications, has a secure job.

This woman of fifty has had 25 years of happy married life, her family growing up around her; another woman is a widow of 50 and is trying to get a job to keep body and soul together.

This man was made a director because he pulled the right strings: another's loyalty and hard work go unrecognised and unrewarded.

This woman has a baby and didn't want it; another would give anything to have a baby and cannot. One man is well thought of by everybody but another has had lies told about him and he has become cynical and bitter.

About these and a hundred more instances it could be truly said: "It isn't fair!"

Personalities are sometimes so deeply hurt by injustice that the scars remain for ever. Nothing scars a child's mind more than injustice. Most children will take punishment when they know they deserve it, but they will remember occasions of injustice all their lives. How important it is, therefore, for parents and teachers to make sure that justice is done — treat a child unjustly and you may inflict lifelong damage.

But injustice is so much a part of our life that we simply

must find a way of dealing with it. So what are we to do? Two things:

First, I believe that the affairs of this world, right down to the most minute detail, are in the hands of a God of Justice. When Abraham was pleading for the righteous remnant in the city of Sodom, he said to God "Shall not the Judge of all the earth do what is just?" The question hardly needs answering — of course God is bound to be just, if not in this world then in the next.

But, you say, you parsons are all the same — always talking about the next world — let's have justice in this world! Fair enough! But then, you see, the next world is as real to me as this one, and I really do believe that the injustices of this world will be rectified in the next. I know that you may find this hard to swallow so let me go on to make a more down-to-earth comment.

Watch the reaction of your own heart. A sense of injustice can rankle within you until it turns you sour. Men become hard and cynical. Women become bitter and bitchy. A Harley Street specialist has said that bitterness can change the very pepsin of your stomach and ruin digestion. A Medical Officer of Health writes of a woman who, during a time when her mind was filled with extreme bitterness, nursed her baby at her breast. An hour or two later the baby died. The MO said that the bitterness caused toxic changes in the breast milk and poisoned the baby.

See how Jesus Christ handled injustice. They told lies about Him. They twisted His words. He was misreported, misrepresented, misunderstood. Innocent though He was He was found guilty on faked evidence and sentenced to death by crucifixion. Pilate, the Roman Governor, spoke for all history when he said, "I find no fault in this man."

But the fact remains that the holiest, gentlest man who ever lived was brutally murdered.

Did He cry "It isn't fair!" No. It is on record that "when He was reviled, He reviled not again, and when He suffered, He threatened not." In the midst of injustice He maintained a noble silence. When they spat in His face, He did not spit back, when they lashed His body with leather, He did not curse them. Instead He said "Father, forgive them ..."

And see what happened to Jesus: He rose above it all and lives for ever to ensure that justice is ultimately done.

If you are smarting under a sense of injustice, don't indulge in self-pity, don't allow bitterness to poison your whole being.

Look at Jesus, the Prince of Life, on whom injustice did its worst, and you will know that the God of all the earth will do what is just, sooner or later.

23

YOURS FOR THE ASKING

HAVE YOU ever dropped a coin down a wishing-well and made a secret wish? Pulled a wish-bone — fairly of course! — and having won the duel, made a wish? When you were very little, did you ever take one of your baby teeth recently extracted with less pain than you cared to admit, and put it under your pillow in the hope that it might turn into a sixpence overnight?

I am not for one moment suggesting that you are superstitious! We have all done this sort of thing. At the time we said it was silly, but I wonder, was it so very silly after all?

I want you to imagine that you have been given a private audience with God Himself, the Maker of Heaven and Earth, the Controller of the Universe. Suppose He were to say to you: "My child, I am able to give you anything I choose. You may make one wish and I will grant it, whatever it may be."

One wish, just one, anything you ask for yours for the taking! What would your wish be?

Would you ask for *money?* "Lord, make me a millionaire!" Well, there is nothing wrong with money. But, you say, the Bible says that money is the root of all evil and they wrote a song about it! But the Bible does not say that money is the root of all evil. What it does say is that *"the love of money* is the root of all kinds of evil."

Do you really want money all that much? Do you honestly think it would solve all your problems?

In a recent newspaper there was an article entitled "How to keep smiling with £714 million." It was about one of the Middle East Oil Kings. It appears that he had flown out from Heathrow that day for his home — he had just heard that one of his children had been taken ill — "I just want to get back home," he said.

Would you wish for *good health?* "Lord, make me strong and healthy." Now that would be a perfectly good and natural wish. Good health is so important. If you have got it, thank God for it.

Perhaps your wish would have to do with your wife, your husband, your children, your sweetheart — only you and God know what it would be.

But I do know about the secret wish of the writer of Psalm 27 in the Bible: "One thing I wish ... that I may dwell in the House of the Lord all the days of my life, to behold the beauty of the Lord, and to inquire in His temple."

This man is not asking God to take him out of the world. He is not asking for the cloistered life. If you take time to read the whole of Psalm 27, you will see that he was very much involved in real life. You see, to dwell on something is to think about it for a long time, to keep returning to the same thoughts again and again. What this man is asking, the one thing for which he wished, was to be right with God, to live a life centred in God, and thus be able to make some sort of sense of what was going on around him.

Can you rise to that sort of wish? The Psalmist who wanted to be right with God was prepared to "seek after it," to work hard for it. He realised, long before the science of psychology came along, that desire is one of the strongest of human emotions.

What do you wish for more than anything else in the whole world? Ask yourself that question now. Better still, let God ask it of you in the quietness of your own heart.

My prayer for you is that you will follow the example of the writer of Psalm 27 and say, "teach me Thy way, O Lord."

24

WHERE TO TAKE YOUR TROUBLES

WHERE DO you turn when in trouble? Knowing where to go with your troubles is one of the most important things in life. Some people have nowhere to turn, which is very sad. Even in this affluent society it is still possible to find people who just don't know where to turn when they are in trouble.

Some people hit the bottle. They turn to drink in the hope that they may find a way of drowning their troubles. Others turn to some other drug in the vain hope that the magic potion will bring peace. They escape — but only for a short time. The problem does not go away. All that happens is that the power to deal with the problem is diminished.

Some turn to other, stronger people. That's good.

Some turn to the Church — and why not? Slip into any city church at any time during the week and you will find people there looking for peace of mind. That is why every church ought to be open even though to leave a church open these days is to risk vandalism. After all, one of the functions of the Church is to comfort people in trouble.

Well, where do *you* turn?

The writer of Psalm 121 begins: "I will lift up mine eyes unto the hills." Then he asks the question: "from whence cometh my help." And then he answers his own question: "My help cometh from the Lord who heaven and earth hath made."

Note that this man looked up to the hills because the hills tell us something about God. They have been there a long time, as long as anybody can remember. Geologists say millions of years — that's a long time. Well, God has been "there" for longer than anybody can remember.

There is a stability about hills. They are not here today and gone tomorrow. Neither is God. And so the writer of this Psalm turns from the hills and finds a God who never changes.

Psalm 121 is known as "The Traveller's Psalm." This is because of some words at the end — "The Lord will bless your going out and your coming in from this time forth and even for evermore."

Going out and coming in — a picture of life.

One of the many things you cannot help noticing about Jesus Christ is that He is always going somewhere. He is "The Pilgrim Christ".

When I walked along the Kidron Valley in Jerusalem I remembered that Jesus walked that way the night before He was nailed to a cross. He had said to His followers, "I am going to my Father." The next day, the Pilgrim Christ walked along the Via Dolorosa ("The Way of Sorrow"), reviled and spat upon as He went by people who had no idea what they were doing. He knew this would happen. He had said "The Son of Man must needs suffer and die."

Being a Christian is following Jesus. It is a pilgrimage. It is going out and coming in, in faith, in the sure and certain belief that Jesus will be with us every step of the way.

I want to say this to you. I believe that God has a purpose for our lives. He is our Father, we are His children. And I believe that in His keeping we can come to no harm.

So we look up to the hills, we press on to the summit, knowing that there is a way through the deep shadows that seem to bar our path at times.

25

USE YOUR IMAGINATION!

A VIEWER has asked for John Lennon's song "Imagine", written in 1972, to be broadcast. Now having listened to "Imagine" I am certain that you will find it thought-provoking. In essence, it is about the possibility of a more perfect world based on the simple things.

You will recall the Beatles' meteoric rise to fame, literally overnight. I can remember their first television broadcast and the immediate impact it made. Their sound was new and exciting (whatever you may have thought at the time!) and resulted in a completely new era of pop music. Beatlemania broke out everywhere! The four Beatles were mobbed wherever they went, their songs rocketed to the top of the hit parade, and they — and many 'hangers-on' — became immensely rich.

The adulation they received was really too much for them; human beings were not meant to be treated as gods; we just haven't got the equipment to handle divinity.

They broke up — it was inevitable — and went their several ways. The adulation, the massive material success, the stress and strain of constantly living in the window of the world for all to see proved too much. In their own ways, they began a search for some sort of reality.

John Lennon turned to Eastern Mysticism for a better world. Of course he did some odd things, odd that is to other people. But why, he argued, couldn't there be peace in the world? Why couldn't the world's hungry be fed? Why couldn't we know something of heaven on earth? And was there anything in all the world more important than love? And so John Lennon wrote "Imagine". One line goes "You may say I'm a dreamer, but I'm not the only one." I think he is one of thousands who, disillusioned with life as it is, dream of something better. And why not?

Imagination is God-given.

Fantasy is something quite different. Fantasy is living in a world of make-believe. It is playing a game that gets nowhere except possibly into escapism.

Imagination is a creative force inherent in everybody. It is the power to see things as they really are, as they were meant to be. When William Blake wrote "And did those feet in ancient time walk upon England's mountains green?" he was using his imagination. This is the function of the poet, the use of this God-given gift of imagination to reach the heart of a world that is all around us.

Jesus Christ used His imagination. When He wanted to demonstrate true beauty, He took a wild flower and said, "consider the lilies of the field. . . ". I am sure that much of our Lord's prayer time was taken up with sanctified imagination. You who are familiar with the neglected art of meditation will know exactly what I mean.

John Lennon's moving song is a cry of the heart for a better and a happier world. But I must say this: Dreaming of a better world is not enough. Imagination of itself is not enough. The world will not get better just by thinking about it. We must do something to help make it better.

For me, and for millions of others, this means following Jesus Christ, doing things His way, giving our imagination to Him.

The world needs dreamers! Remember — "no star is ever lost we once have seen, we always may be what we might have been."

26

A LANTERN FOR MY CHRIST

JUST a mile off the busy A30 which carries an ever-increasing volume of traffic between London and Cornwall there is a place of infinite peace — the little Church of St Peter at Lew Trenchard.

There is a quiet here broken only by the song of the birds and the hum of the bees in the great lime trees. Here we can pause for a moment and feel about us something of that older, more peaceful England whose rhythms were based on the eternal things, on sunrise and sunset, on seed time and harvest.

St Petrock, the great Welsh missionary who converted much of Devon and Cornwall in the 6th century was Patron Saint of Lew Trenchard Church before its re-dedication to St. Peter in the 13th century. At the end of the 19th century a major restoration was begun by the Rev. Sabine Baring-Gould who said that it was his life ambition to make of the little church what he called "A Lantern for my Christ."

Almost everyone in the parish of Lew Trenchard could tell you the story of this remarkable man's life. He was a 'Squarson", that is to say he was both Squire and Parson, one of the last, if not the last of his kind.

They will tell you how he fell passionately in love with a Yorkshire mill girl at Horbury Brig where he was curate, how he sent her to a finishing school to be educated where she remained but six months, such was Sabine's anxiety to get wed! The story of how Sabine and Grace fell in love and married is worthy to be set alongside the great romances of all time. She bore him fifteen children!

Of course his family said that he had "married beneath

him," but they were to be proved wrong.

Sabine Baring-Gould had a great respect for the past. At the same time he was a man who was often in advance of his own time. For instance, he was more of a European than an Englishman. You can see evidence of this in the church itself where you will find work by craftsmen from France, Belgium, Switzerland and Germany.

He was a hymn-writer. He wrote "Now the day is over", that lovely children's hymn, and "Through the night of doubt and sorrow", a hymn for pilgrims.

But his greatest hymn is "Onward! Christian Soldiers, marching as to war, with the Cross of Jesus going on before." What I like about this hymn is its militant note. For too long, the Church has been on the defensive and Christians have been on the defensive, almost apologising for their faith. I think it is time we went over to the offensive and spoke out forthrightly against the evils of our day — we would gain far more respect that way.

St Paul was very much aware of the fact that the Christian life is a battle. We fight it out on two fronts, he said — within ourselves where the battle for personal purity and integrity is going on all the time; and outside ourselves in the community of which we are a part, where so many forces are arrayed against us.

So if you should find yourself on the A30 near Lew Down, make for Lew Trenchard and step inside its little church. If you are quiet enough you may just hear the angels singing "Onward! Christian Soldiers, marching as to war, with the Cross of Jesus going on before."

27

THE CHAIN LETTER

I RECEIVED a chain letter recently. It was headed "Think a Prayer", and indeed begins with a prayer. It then went on to say: "This prayer has been sent to you for good luck. It has been round the world nine times. The luck has been sent to you. You are to receive good luck within four days of receiving this letter. It is no joke. You will receive it in the mail."

Then the letter went on to instruct me to send twenty copies to people "you think need good luck. Do not keep this letter. It must leave within 96 hours after you receive it." But what will happen if I fail to carry out the instructions?

This was where the letter became threatening.

A certain General failed to do as the letter told him and it was claimed that he lost his wife by death six days later. Someone else received the letter, and, not believing in it, threw it away — it was said that he died nine days later. An office clerk got the letter and forgot about it. A few days later he lost his job. Then he remembered the letter, sent out twenty copies and got a better job! At least, so it was claimed!

I want to tell you in the strongest language that such a letter is dangerous nonsense. The people who start these chain letters are either downright wicked or sick, probably both. The letter is right about one thing when it says "It is no joke."

Certainly it is no joke for some of the people to whom it is sent. I can imagine them being deeply disturbed by it.

The most pathetic part of the letter I received was a postscript added by the sender, someone who lives at

Trowbridge. "I apologise for sending the enclosed to you. These letters are very distressing for some people to receive, and I wish I had the courage to throw mine into the bin. But I do not, and my only way out seems to post my twenty to folk who will have the strength to do what I cannot."

Have no truck with this nonsense! Be strong-minded enough to destroy it the moment you get it.

"Think a Prayer" indeed! What a travesty of real prayer! Do people really think that prayer is a kind of fruit machine into which you put a coin and find you've won the jackpot? This is mere superstition.

If you really want to know what prayer is all about, read what Jesus Christ has to say about it in His famous Sermon on the Mount. You will find it in St Matthew, chapter six.

Jesus says three things:

True prayer does not consist in the saying of words. "Do not go babbling on like the heathen" is what Jesus actually says.

Neither is prayer something you do aloud at street corners for all to hear — prayer is inward and secret and private.

And in any event, Jesus says "your Father knows what your needs are before you ask Him."

Then Jesus taught His disciples the greatest prayer in all the world — "Our Father, which art in heaven, hallowed be Thy name..."

Chain letters make me angry because they prey on the simple-minded and the sick, and because they present a completely false picture of the God to whom we pray.

We have deviated so far from true religion that we don't recognise lies about God when we hear them. It is high time we took another and a longer look at what Jesus Christ really does say about life.

28

RICHARD'S REMEDY

AMONG the letters I receive was one from a young man of eighteen. I found it so stimulating and challenging and moving that I quote from it. It came from Richard, eighteen-years-old, who tells me very frankly why he doesn't go to church.

He begins by saying that as a boy he went to a Methodist Sunday School, and that later when he reached his teens he attended Evensong in his Parish Church. Of Evensong he writes: "I found it had little or nothing to offer. One goes through a series of psalms, then the Vicar reads off his sermon. When one looks around, the church is seen to contain a few old people, mostly women. Inevitably nowadays, churches are empty, except when the TV cameras are about!"

Richard goes on to say that he has attended Mass in a Roman Catholic Church which he found "very romantic but hard to understand."

"On the whole," he writes, "the Church has little or nothing to offer a young person." Then he refers to the church door as "that forbidding door. I suspect that only a few who are in dire need of help and spiritual guidance would walk through that door alone when young."

He says that he understands the clergy's anxiety about the decline in church attendance — the best way, naturally, is to get through to the young. And then he says something that made me stop and think: "The worst possible way is to seem as if they are selling religion at a bargain offer of 4p off type of thing. Young people don't want this, I am sure. They laugh at guitars in church — it doesn't belong."

Richard's remedy?

"Rip down the musty doors and replace them with glass so that all the world can see what's going on inside. Simplify the sermons! Put them into everyday language, cut out long tedious words that sound good but mean nothing."

And then this cry of the heart from this young man:

"People of my age need faith for life when we suddenly break through the barriers of adolescence and learn of bombs and suffering and starvation. We realise our little world of teddy bears and dolls wasn't true, and our world comes tumbling down on top of us. We certainly need a faith. This is when we need to be shown the way."

Richard reckons that Lust is the biggest sin for young people of his own age — "not just lust for women, but lust for money." He takes a pessimistic view of the future: "I hate to admit it, but mine may well be the last generation to inherit the earth."

Those are just a few of the challenging things Richard said in his long and interesting letter which I found helpfully disturbing.

I accept the criticism Richard levels at much that passes for worship in our churches, and I am absolutely certain he is right when he says that young people won't fall for the soft-sell approach — they want to be challenged as Jesus challenged His disciples — "take up your cross daily and follow me."

Nevertheless, I believe that these things need to be said from *inside* the Church. And we must never despise the older folk found in our churches, for without their faithful and devoted service over the years the Church of Christ would be a lot poorer.

Nor must it be supposed that every church is practically empty. Some are well-filled every Sunday. And if you take the world view, it is a fact that the Christian Church is getting bigger every day.

Richard takes a pessimistic view of the future. He isn't

the first. St Paul thought the world was coming to an end two thousand years ago. Even so, there is a lot in what Richard wrote.

29

WHAT A REVIVAL WOULD DO FOR BRITAIN

VERY FEW people have ever taken Christianity seriously.

Certainly no nation has ever truly based its way of life upon the teaching of Jesus Christ. Our own country is a so-called Christian country. We talk about the ethos of our national life being Christian. We claim that our parliamentary system of government, our democratic way of doing things, our educational system are all Christian in foundation. The House of Commons has its chaplain. Most local Councils begin their deliberations with prayers. At many luncheon and dinner functions, grace is said before the meal, provided a parson happens to be present!

All this is true, but who is going to claim that Britain is a Christian country?

This is the land of occasional religion. It takes some great national disaster to lift a lid in our minds which we normally keep shut. We come over religious at Christmas. We come over religious at Easter. But for the rest of the time, the teaching of Jesus Christ is conveniently left alone.

Just suppose that a revival of true religion took place in this country; just suppose that we really began to take Christ seriously; what would a revival do for Britain? It would bring a sense of purpose into our working lives.

On all sides you hear responsible people saying "we don't work hard enough as a nation." The politicians and the economists tell us that if we are to get more out of the economy by way of higher wages we must put more in by way of production.

But you cannot make people work harder by legislation. They've got to want to work harder, and they have to see why they should work harder. If work is about wages and nothing more, it is no wonder there are so many strikes and industrial disputes. Christianity says that the true motive behind work is the making of a worthy contribution to the well-being of the whole world, not forgetting the under-privileged.

Taking Christianity seriously would bring down the number of divorces. I am not saying that divorce is unacceptable in a Christian community. Jesus Himself said it was permissible in certain circumstances. But what I am saying is that the attitude to marriage in this country is less than Christian. Marriage has to be worked at if it is to be reasonably successful. You cannot go running off the moment something goes wrong.

Taking Christianity seriously would raise our moral standards. They need to be raised. A headmaster speaking at his school's speech day recently said that young people today are fed up with the double standards of so many adults. Young people, he said, see things in black and white, but they quickly learn that our society has many shades of grey — honesty was a shade of grey, integrity, conscientiousness was a shade of grey.

But why should anybody be moral? What is the point? There is no point apart from religion, none whatever.

Taking Christianity seriously would restore a sense of greatness to our nation. Once this nation led the world. Now because of the tremendous growth of other nations we no longer wield the influence we once did in world affairs. But we could still be great. The world needs a moral and spiritual lead, and we could give that lead if only we ourselves were morally and spiritually equipped to do so.

Mind you, the price is high, too high for most. It would mean living a life with others at the centre instead of self. This is what Jesus did. This is real Christianity. And it is the only way to make life really worth-while. Are you a Christian?

30

THE BREAD OF LIFE

EVERYBODY loves a Harvest Festival Service — the church is crowded, the hymns are bright, and there, at the heart of the harvest decorations is the time-honoured harvest loaf in the shape of a sheaf of wheat. There is considerable artistry in getting the shape of the sheaf just right — a credit to the local baker who made it. You can see the ears of corn, the straw binding round the middle, and at the bottom a little field mouse with currants for eyes!

Bread — the staff of life. Do you know where wheat was first cultivated? About seven thousand years ago on the eastern seaboard of the Mediterranean Sea wheat grew wild. Man tamed it and cultivated the crop we know today. And, of course, a part of the eastern seaboard of the Mediterranean is the Holy Land where Jesus Christ lived His earthly life. They call this part of the Middle East "The Fertile Crescent," and it was here, where wheat was first tamed, that the "Bread of Life" came down from heaven.

"I am the bread of life," He said, and not long after He fed the Five Thousand with our sort of bread. But surely what He was really saying was that we need more than our kind of bread if we are to be whole people — we need spiritual food as well, and this He is able to give us.

There is something about bread in the Lord's Prayer: "Give us this day our daily bread." Notice that it is "give *us*," and not "give *me*". This is a prayer for the whole world. If you are a Christian, you cannot pray "Give me my daily bread and let the rest of the world go hungry."

But a great part of the world is hungry. Last year

thirty-one million people died of hunger, many of them little children.

This need not be. Scientists tell us that if we applied our scientific knowledge to the production of food on a world scale, there would be enough for everybody, and some to spare.

We waste food — a lot of it — and this is a sin. When I was in Cornwall I saw a field of spring cabbage. I asked when they would be marketed. "I shall not bother," said the farmer. And then he told me that he would get 20p a box if he sent them to London, and a box contained 48lbs — you and I were paying about half that *per pound* in the shops at the time.

I don't blame the Cornish farmer. It just wasn't worth his while to harvest the crop. But there is something very wrong with a system that allows good food to go to waste. And this happens on a much bigger scale all over the world to keep prices artificially high. It's a sin.

There is a story about a village squire and one of the villagers. Mrs Hodge had just given birth to her fifth child. The squire met her in the street and duly congratulated her. "You know, Mrs Hodge," he said, "the Lord never sends a mouth without he sends the bread to fill it."

"Well sir," she said, "I can't help noticing that He sends all the mouths to my house and all the bread to yours!"

World hunger and all its ugly consequences is the biggest single problem in the world today. The Christian solution is for the "Haves" to share with the "Have-nots". It's the only way.

Just before He was murdered, Jesus shared a meal with His friends. They had often eaten together. But this meal was different. He took a loaf of bread (rather like a cottage loaf), said grace over it, broke it into small pieces, and then gave a piece to each of His friends, with these immortal words:

"This is my body, given for you. Take, eat."

Bread for a hungry world. Bread to pilgrims given. And all who eat of this Bread live for ever!

31

THE TOUCH OF CHRIST

PERHAPS it has come as a surprise to some to learn that leprosy still claims victims today –– we might have been tempted to think that it was a disease that disappeared long ago.

In Jesus Christ's day the leper was an all-too-common sight. A combination of poverty and squalor created the conditions in which such diseases ran riot.

The leper was cut off from the rest of society. By law, because of the contagious nature of the disease, he had to keep away from all other human beings lest they might themselves contract the disease. And just in case people got too close to him he was obliged to wear a bell round his neck to warn others of his plight. And if that were not enough he would have to cry out "unclean, unclean!" if anyone got too close. What a terrible state to be in!

What happened to such a man? Well, he was registered as a leper, came under the oversight of the priest, and died a slow dreadful death.

The leper I want to tell you about had heard of Jesus Christ. When he knew that the Man of Nazareth was coming his way he made up his mind to intercept Him. "If you want to," he shouted to Jesus, "you can cure me and make me clean!"

There's faith for you — a leper believing that Jesus could cure him of a disease that the best medical opinion said was incurable!

"All right," said Jesus, "I will cure you."

Now note what follows. Jesus reached out His hand and touched the leper, and immediately the man was healed. He was cured, he was clean, a leper no longer.

What was it that brought about the cure? Was it the physical touch of Jesus? Some think that it was, that the very touch of Jesus was vibrant with health-giving qualities capable of healing the sick. I am sure this is a part of the truth — we have all heard of people who possess healing power in their hands.

But there was more, far more to it than that. As far as the leper was concerned, the fact that Jesus touched him meant more than he would ever be able to put into words.

It was the touch of understanding. Jesus knew how this man felt, what being cut off from his family and friends meant. This is what is so true about Jesus Christ; He understands people better than anybody else does. "He knew what was in man."

By touching this leper Jesus became one with him. In the eyes of the Law anyone who touched a leper, whether deliberately or accidentally, automatically rendered himself unclean and was obliged to go to the priest (who was also a surgeon) to be cleansed. So Jesus, in touching this man, said in effect, "I am in this with you."

Do you see what this must have meant to this man? Here was the Great Healer, the one everybody was talking about, actually touching him! It was the touch of hope.

The medical profession of the day said that this man's condition was hopeless, that his illness was terminal. The best he could do was to make sure that no one else caught the disease from him. Jesus gave him hope — hope for the hopeless!

In this impersonal, dehumanising society, where human dignity tends to mean less and less, we need the personal, life-giving, hopeful touch of Christ, the Christ who teaches that every human being matters to God, that human life is precious, that all life is to be reverenced.

We can know the touch of Christ today. And we can pass it on to others.

There is a hymn we sometimes sing in church on

Sunday evenings—"At even 'ere the sun was set." This is how the last verse goes:

> Thy touch hath still its ancient power,
> No word from Thee can fruitless fall:
> Hear in this solemn evening hour,
> And in Thy mercy heal us all.

32

FOLLOW THAT STAR!

BENEATH the Church of the Holy Nativity at Bethlehem is a basement known as "The Stables". This, it is said, is the place where Jesus was born. There being no room for the Holy Family in the inn, Mary's Boy Child was born in a stable.

Set within the mosaic of the floor is a star — the Star of Bethlehem, to remind us that Wise Men followed a star and found Jesus Christ.

The stars have always held a fascination for people. Somehow, it is thought, our destiny is linked to the stars. That must be why millions read their horoscopes in their daily newspapers!

The stars had a fascination for the ancients. When a new star appeared — or one they had not seen before — they assumed it was a portent of some very special event. Poets have found the stars a rich subject for the imagination.

I was in the RAF during the War, and I recall thinking hard about the RAF motto, "Per Ardua ad Astra" — "through hardships to the stars". I thought then, and still think, that that motto contains profound truth, for it is often necessary to endure hardship on the way to the highest.

For some reason those who reach the top of their profession in show business are called stars. From time to time you read that somebody has become "a star overnight". I doubt it. Read the life story of the star and you will probably find that long before stardom was achieved there were many years of hard work before the magic moment came. A writer may slog away for years, writing articles and novels that bring very little response from his readers, then suddenly one novel does it and he is famous.

This is very true of our spiritual pilgrimage. A contemporary writer said of Jesus Christ, "Son though He was, yet He learned by all that he suffered." We shall never know just how much Jesus suffered. But we do know that only through suffering did he redeem the world.

The most balanced people I know, the most whole people I know, are those men and women who have really gone through troubles, who have really experienced the hardships of life and have come through to the stars.

In Revelation 12, there is a strange picture: "And there appeared a great wonder in heaven; a woman clothed with the sun, and the moon under her feet, and upon her head a crown of twelve stars:"

I suppose that this is where the saying "another star in your crown" comes from.

A star is a thing of mystery. What is a star? What is it made of? And even when the scientists have told us exactly what the stars are made of, and how they got to be where they are, to us ordinary folk they remain a mystery. Partly because we need mystery. Our souls need mystery. We need the stars to lift us out of the world of earthy things.

A star is a thing of hope. We say "hitch your wagon to a star." Have something to aim for, to reach after. Stretch out your hands and take a star!

But often it is hard to reach the stars. "Through troubles to the stars." An aeroplane takes off into the wind. Face the wind and rise to the stars.

There is another way. When I was a boy on a farm in Bideford, North Devon, our roads were full of tramps. They called often at the farm and were always met with kindness by my parents. One was asked if he planned his route in advance? "No," he said, "when I wake up in the morning, I wets my finger and holds it up to feel which way the wind is blowing. Then I puts my back to it and walks on!"

The Star of Bethlehem heralded the Birth of Christ, the Morning Star. Follow that star!

33

WATER INTO WINE!

IF YOU have been to a wedding lately you will have heard the minister refer to marriage as that "holy estate which Christ sanctioned and adorned with His presence, and first miracle that He wrought in Cana of Galilee. . ." — wonderful words, aren't they?

I have been to Cana. It is just down the road from Nazareth on the way to the Sea of Galilee. It was at Cana that Jesus turned water into wine at a wedding feast. The story is told by St John in his Gospel. Now, when St John tells a story, it has two meanings — the ordinary everyday meaning, plus a deeper meaning for those who have a mind to understand it.

It would seem that Mary the Mother of Jesus was in charge of the catering arrangements, for it was to Mary that the servants came with the alarming news that the wine had run out. We have to remember that for a Jewish feast, wine was essential. "Without wine," said the Rabbis, "there is no joy."

Mary at once told Jesus what had happened. She then told the servants to do exactly what Jesus told them. And they did. At His command they filled six large jars with water, and then found to their astonishment that the water had been turned into wine. In fact, so good was the wine that the guests said, "You have kept the best wine until now."

There have been many ingenious attempts to explain away this miracle. Some have tried to say that the guests were so far gone that they couldn't distinguish water from wine! That's hardly likely! But why should it be thought remarkable that He who made the universe should be able to turn water into wine? Why quibble about it?

Far better, I think, to ask what it means for us today, for you see, Jesus never performed a miracle for His own sake, never to show off, but always for the sake of others.

So what is this miracle all about?

First note that it happened at a wedding. A wedding is meant to be a happy occasion. Yes, I know the bride's mother and most of the womenfolk shed a tear or two, but that's because they are happy! A wedding is a happy time. And here is Jesus working His first miracle at a wedding, and surely this means that religion is meant to be a thing of joy.

Somehow or other, the idea has got about that if you are a Christian, you have to deny yourself everything that is joyous and bright and happy, and put on a long face and black clothes and talk like an undertaker.

Let's remember that Jesus was the Man of Joys, the Radiant Christ who came to make people happy, not miserable. And yet some Christians look as if they were baptised in vinegar!

Note *where* it happened — in an ordinary home in a remote part of the world. Not in a palace against the background of some great occasion. You see, Jesus brought religion into the ordinary things of life. And *why* did He do it? Well, hospitality was a sacred duty to the Jew and still is. If the wine had run out and no more had been forthcoming, that Galilean family would never have lived it down. Jesus acted as He did to save them humiliation.

But for me the most striking part of the story is the attitude of Mary. When she was told that things had gone wrong she at once turned to Jesus. She knew her Son better than anybody. After all, she had lived with Him for thirty years.

There is a lovely old legend that tells of the days when Jesus was a small baby at Nazareth, which says that when people felt tired and upset, they would say "Let's go and look at Mary's Child." And when they did, their troubles rolled away.

And remember what Mary said to the servants — "Whatever He tells you to do, do it." She knew that whatever He said would be right. You and I need to show the same simple confident faith in the Lord of Life.

34

TOLERANCE

IT MAY not be thought inappropriate if I say something about tolerance. By tolerance I mean, a disposition of mind that allows other people to hold views different from our own, especially religious beliefs.

Religion is a potentially explosive subject. It can generate a vast amount of heat. It can lead people to do and say things calculated to do great harm to the cause of Christianity. It has led to bloodshed and strife of the bitterest kind. This is a negation of the Spirit of Christ. Our Lord is crucified afresh every time Christians come together in bitter conflict.

I am a Methodist. I am grateful for my Methodist heritages. But I do not subscribe to the view that the Methodist Church has a monopoly of the truth because I know that such a position is untenable.

Without wishing to appear in the least patronising, let me tell you what I believe we can learn from other parts of the Christian church.

We can learn a lot from the Roman Catholics — their devotion, their intense love of their Lord, their emphasis upon the redemptive nature of the death of Chirst. I recall a Midlands housewife telling me that she would be at Mass at six o'clock the following morning. "That's no picnic," I said. "And Calvary wasn't a picnic either," she replied.

And how thankful we ought to be for the Church of England. The way the Established Church has influenced the State and maintained a Christian witness in the high places of our land, the beauty of the Prayer Book services — not least the music — and the magnificent buildings

Faith for Life

that bear a silent witness to the things of God in town and country.

And what about the Salvation Army, those brave soldiers of Jesus Christ who witness to their faith in the open-air in all weathers when the rest of us are cloistered, who take the Gospel into the pubs, who serve the poor and needy wherever they may be found, and who provide a home for the homeless when every other door is shut? We have a lot to learn from the Salvation Army.

Then there are the Pentecostalists with their emphasis upon the power of the Holy Spirit; the Christian Brethren with their witness to the Bible as the Word of God; the Quakers with their sacramental concept of life; and the many other smaller sects and denominations, each bearing witness to some aspect of the truth about God.

There is not a single branch of the Christian Church that has not made some contribution to Christian Truth as a whole. By the same token, every denomination can learn something from every other. We need to be tolerant of one another's views.

But I will tell you what has happened — all of us have been so taken up with stating and defending our own entrenched positions that we have taken our eyes off the One who matters most, Jesus Christ.

You will recall that the twelve Apostles were remarkably different in all sorts of ways. In fact, it would be difficult to find a group of men who differed more than did the Apostles. Among them were an employer and an employee, representatives of Right and Left politically speaking, at least one agnostic, and temperamental differences galore. In the ordinary course of events they would never have come together. And yet these same men were welded into such a force as was to turn the world upside down. Only Jesus Christ could have worked such a miracle.

I am all for Church Unity. I cannot tell you how disappointed I was in 1971 when the Anglicans and the

Methodists failed to agree on a scheme of union. Unity will come, of that I am sure. In the meantime, let us learn the grace of tolerance.

It is perhaps worth remembering that the Methodist Church was founded by an Anglican (John Wesley) and the Salvation Army by a Methodist (William Booth)!

35

SUN WORSHIPPERS

MOST OF US are interested in ancient monuments. They hold up a mirror to the past.

By far the most interesting monument in England is Stonehenge. In the 18th century it was thought that Stonehenge had been a temple for the devotions of the Druids, the priests of the Celtic Ancient Britons. This romantic view became widespread, so much so that nowadays a group of people calling themselves Druids gather at the site each year at daybreak on Midsummer Day.

The outer circle of stones, from which many are missing, has a diameter of 100 feet. Sixteen stones remain, most of them standing 14 feet above the ground, and each weighing approximately 26 tons. Inside the outer ring is another circle of stones, again incomplete. Inside this again come two further groups of stones, horseshoe in shape. At the very centre is the great "hele stone", named after the Greek word "helios" which means "sun".

When you visit Stonehenge and look up at those huge stones in the inner circles, you wonder how on earth they got there. Geologists say they are identical with the stones found in Pembrokeshire, two hundred miles away.

It could be that Stonehenge was there long before the Druids came on the scene, but the one thing that seems certain is that it is a great pre-historic sanctuary in some way connected with sun-worship.

I am not at all surprised that the Ancient Britons worshipped the sun. They were wrong in believing that the sun was a god, but they were right in believing that there would not have been life on this planet but for the sun. If the light of the sun was cut off, everyone would perish from cold and starvation. In fact, if the heat of the sun were reduced by only 10% the whole of the temperate zone would be converted into frozen wastes.

The Bible has a lot to say about the sun. In the very first chapter we are told that God created the sun — "that greater light to rule the day." In the Book of Deuteronomy the Jews are warned against sun-worship. Joshua is reported to have told the sun to "stand still." Even Joshua, it appears, had an inflated idea of his own importance! Hezekiah is said to have made the sun go backwards— a pretty impressive trick to have up your sleeve!

Jesus once used the sun to bring home a very important truth. "Your heavenly Father makes the sun to rise on the good and the bad." Divine impartiality. The good are not given preferential treatment. God has no favourites. The bad receive the blessing of God even though they may never return thanks.

St Paul, when preaching practical Christianity to the members of the Church at Ephesus, had this to say: "Let not the sun go down upon your anger." Make it up before sundown!

But the sun receives its most honourable mention in a speech made by Zechariah, the father of John the Baptist. His son, he said, would be called "the Prophet of the Highest", because he was to be the forerunner of Jesus Christ. And speaking of Jesus, as yet unborn, Zechariah had this to say: "The Morning Sun will rise upon us, to shine on those who live in darkness."

That is the Sun I worship — Jesus Christ, the Light of the World, day and night!

36

STRANGE GOINGS-ON ON
HUMPTY DUMPTY HILL

ALL KINDS of curious customs are associated with Hallowe'en, a mixture of pagan and religious traditions. The Romans celebrated Hallowe'en and the Celts made it their New Year's Eve. People used to light bonfires on Hallowe'en to ward off any evil spirit that might be lurking in the darkness, for this is the night when witches are supposed to be out on their broomsticks!

In Lancashire they call it Duck-Apple Night, when the game of bobbing for apples in a bowl of water is played. It is not unkown, even today, for a girl to eat an apple in front of a mirror at midnight on the chance that the apparition of her future husband will appear over her shoulder. In Scotland, and some parts of England, grotesque lanterns are made out of hollowed out turnips, so adding to the spine-chilling atmosphere.

According to a newspaper report there have been some ghostly goings-on at Humpty Dumpty Hill at Northam in North Devon. The people who live on its new housing estate complained of things going bump in the night, crockery and ornaments being shattered mysteriously, ghostly figures going up and down stairs. A little boy has told of "strangely dressed soldiers in his bedroom." The local vicar has been called in to exorcise these mischievous spirits.

Apparently, the houses on Humpty Dumpty Hill are built on what many local people believe is an old burial ground. One lady is reported to have said, "We believe there could be a link." Perhaps.

Of course, the Christian meaning of Hallowe'en is that there is a union — a spiritual union — between the living and the dead. The Church believes in the Communion of Saints. That is to say, in a real union between the Church on earth (the Church Militant) and the Church in heaven (the Church Triumphant).

The evidence to support belief in the existence of another world leaves no room for doubt. Apart from what Christians themselves believe, serious psychic research has produced an immense amount of evidence in support of this belief.

For me the final authority in this and all matters is Jesus Christ.

One day, Jesus took three of His disciples, Peter, James and John, up a mountain. He had done this sort of thing before to refresh His own spirit as well as theirs. But this was to be different. In the early dawn, something happened to the appearance of Jesus that we have since come to know as Transfiguration. He was praying, and as they looked at Him, the disciples realised that a great light was shining out from behind His eyes in a way they had never noticed before.

Then something else happened. Two men, long dead, were seen talking with Jesus. They were Moses and Elijah. The Bible says that the three disciples were "terrified" — I am not surprised! Wouldn't you have been? The question is — were Moses and Elijah really there? Or were the disciples seeing things?

I believe they were really there. To me it seems a perfectly natural thing for such a spiritually-minded person as Jesus to converse with the spiritual giants of the past. They are kindred spirits. Hallowe'en says it can happen.

There is the story of a Roman Catholic priest returning from Mass early one morning. Only a handful of people had been there. A farmer, fetching in the cows for morning milking, called out "How many did you have in church this morning, Father?" The priest replied, "millions, my son, millions!"

37

MEMORY MONTH

NOVEMBER has been called "Memory Month". On the fifth we remember the man who tried, unsuccessfully, to raise the Houses of Parliament to a higher level in the infamous Gunpowder Plot. Also on the fifth we remember that this is the anniversary of the landing of William of Orange at Brixham.

On the second Sunday in November, by order of the Queen, we remember the men and women who lost their lives in two World Wars.

The first of November is a Christian Festival — that of All Saints. It was on this very day that Martin Luther nailed his Theses to the church door at Wittenberg, and thus inaugurated the Reformation.

The Church has a symbol to depict All Saints. It is very simple in design — a golden crown on a red background, signifying the victory won by the saints over evil. The word "sanctus" appears three times under the golden crown, a word meaning "holy". In the Book of Revelation, we read that the saints in heaven chanted "Holy, Holy, Holy, is God the Sovereign Lord of all."

And so, on All Saints Day, Christians remember those tens of thousands who were slaughtered because they dared to name Jesus Christ as their Lord and Saviour. In the early days of the Christian Church many were martyred for their faith. The Romans had made Emperor Worship compulsory, and anyone who refused to worship the Emperor was put to death publicly and cruelly. It was Caesar or Christ, and those who chose Christ paid for it with their lives.

Of course, some of the martyrdom stories have been exaggerated. But there is no such exaggeration in the story of Perpetua.

Perpetua was a young woman of 22. She came from a good family, was well-educated, and was a married woman with a newborn babe. She was a Christian and said so without hesitation. Because of her Christian beliefs she was arrested and thrown into prison.

She admits she was terrified. The stench and heat of the crowded cell was overpowering. Happily she was moved to a smaller cell where she was able to suckle her child. She writes: "The prison was to me a palace where I would rather have been than anywhere else." When brought before the judge she was ordered to sacrifice to the Emperor. She refused and so was condemned with her Christian comrades to fight the beasts. She writes "So we went with joy to our prison."

Perpetua's heathen father did his utmost to persuade his daughter to save her life. And there was the babe at her breast. Even at her trial her father called out, "Daughter, have pity on my grey hairs, have compassion on thy father." To which Perpetua answered, "I can call myself by no other name than Christian."

And so she went to her death in the arena, first horribly gored by an incensed bull, then finally put to death by a gladiator's sword to the cheers of the blood-thirsty mob.

She passed over, all the trumpets sounding for her on the other side as they have done for all the saints who from their labours rest.

Isaac Watts, the great hymn-writer, writing about the saints, has this to say:

"I ask them whence their victory came.
    They, with united breath,
Ascribe their conquest to the Lamb,
    Their triumph, to His death.
They marked the footsteps that He trod,
    His zeal inspired their breast;
And, following their incarnate God,
    Possess the promised rest".

The blood of the martyrs is the seed of the Church! Memory month indeed!

(Over several years the author presented a very popular religious programme late on Sunday nights under the title "Songs of Zion." The format was simple — a hymn played at the request of a viewer, and the telling of the story behind the hymn. It was thought that readers might wish to recall some of those talks).

38

"PEACE, PERFECT PEACE"

A VIEWER wrote to tell me of his experiences in the First World War. The war was bloody and life was cheap. His comrades were dying all round him. Whatever happened you couldn't be sure you would be alive to tell the tale tomorrow. And home was a million muddy miles away. It was then, this viewer told me, that he realised for the first time the reality of the message of that lovely hymn "Peace, perfect peace, in this dark world of sin? The blood of Jesus whispers peace within." It was, he says, something to hold on to.

This hymn was written by a former Bishop of Exeter, Dr Bickersteth. He wrote it on a Sunday in August, 1875. That morning he had heard a sermon preached on the text: "Thou wilt keep him in perfect peace whose mind is stayed on Thee." (Isaiah: 26:3).

The preacher had referred to the phrase "perfect peace" and had explained that when a Hebrew wanted to stress the importance of a word, he repeated it, and that originally this text read "peace, peace". It was this point that rivetted itself on Dr Bickersteth's mind and all the way home he was thinking about it.

That afternoon, the Bishop visited a dying relative, and, finding him very troubled in mind, Dr Bickersteth took a sheet of paper and there and then wrote his hymn "Peace, perfect peace". He then read it to the dying man who was greatly comforted.

I wonder if you have noticed that the first line of every verse of this hymn is in fact a question? Very few people have noticed this. Instead, they sing each line as a statement of fact and so lose the real meaning of the words. Take this verse:

Question: "Peace, perfect peace, by thronging duties pressed?"

Answer: "To do the will of Jesus, this is rest."

Remember that the Bishop did not write this hymn in the quiet of his study as some sort of intellectual exercise. You might be inclined to say that it is all very well for a parson to talk about the perfect peace in a world like this, and that what he ought to do is to come out from his ivory tower and live in the real world for a bit. Fair enough! But the Bishop wrote this hymn to comfort a dying man — that is a real enough situation.

There was no time to consult the Bible, no time to pull down a book from his study shelves. What he wrote that Sunday afternoon came from his heart. It was a simple affirmation of the faith that believes that this is God's world, that God is in control, and that at the end of the day, no matter how long and dark it may be, God's Will be done. Dr Bickersteth took Jesus at His word when He said "My peace I give unto you."

Well, what is Peace?

Is it what you get when the children are safely off to school in the morning, or tucked up in bed at night, and you have a few minutes for yourself?

Is it what you get on holiday, away from a telephone that never stops ringing and a life that just never stops?

Both kinds of peace are worth having, but neither is the peace of which this hymn speaks. There is a lovely benediction in the Bible that goes like this: "The peace of God that passes all human understanding, keep your heart and mind in the knowledge and love of God".

The peace of God is a positive thing. It isn't just the absence of noise, nor is it the absence of problems and difficulties. As a matter of fact, it is the kind of peace you can know in the midst of a storm.

They tell me that way down below the surface of the ocean there are waters that remain undisturbed by even the fiercest storm on the surface.

You cannot buy this peace. You cannot earn it.

You cannot learn it. But you can receive it from the Prince of Peace Himself, which is why a Bishop, challenged to comfort a dying man, wrote down seven fundamentals about life and answered them all with the one word — JESUS,

Peace be with you!

39

"ALL CREATURES OF OUR GOD AND KING"

ONE of the world's great hymns of praise was written more than 700 years ago by St Francis of Assisi, and translated from Latin to English by Dr Draper about 70 years ago. Dr Draper's version of this hymn came out of Yorkshire, and like Baring-Gould's "Onward! Christian Soldiers", was first written for a children's festival.

St Francis taught us a very important lesson — that we should love the simple things of life and praise God for them.

Outside the little town of Assisi in Italy, there is a group of buildings called St Damian. There, on a summer day in July, 1225, came St Francis ill, blind and lonely, knowing he would get comfort from the Poor Clares (whose Order he had instituted), and especially from his friend, St Clare. The quiet courtyard of St Damian, which has altered little since, was a haven of rest, and there St Francis, in his brown habit and sandalled feet, sat down. The Sisters built a cell of reeds in the garden so that St Francis could be undisturbed. At night he found it difficult to sleep because an army of mice ran over his face. Each day he would go up to the house for his meals. Soon the Poor Clares noticed that his old gaiety was returning.

"A single sunbeam," he would say, "is enough to drive away many shadows."

It was at this time that St Francis wrote "All creatures of our God and King." He called it his "Canticle of the Sun", and this beatitude of praise has become the prototype of hymns of praise throughout the world.

St Francis was born into a wealthy family. As a youth he loved the bright lights, spending in a night what would have kept most people for a month. At the age of nineteen he joined the Army and was soon taken prisoner; but even in prison he became known and loved for his kindness and gaiety. On his release he gave up his old life and, as he put it, "embraced Sister Poverty."

He had a great capacity for loving everybody and everything that God had made. He loved "Dear Mother Earth, who day by day, unfoldest blessings on our way, O praise Him, Alleluia!"

St Francis was known as "The Little Poor Man", but in another sense he was the richest of men. He gave his natural gaiety to God and was in fact known to many as "The Jester of the Lord". Often he would laugh and sing for the sheer joy of living.

There are many delightful legends about Francis and the animals. Believing as he did that all creatures are God's creatures, he talked to the animals as much as to human beings. There is the famous sermon he preached to the birds, to which they are said to have listened "in reverent quiet". The fish are said to have swum to the river bank for his blessing. The pheasants of Siena are said to have pined away when he died. And there is the story of the wolf which he converted to gentleness.

St Francis addressed animals, plants, the elements and even inanimate things as "brother" and "sister" because he saw them all as diverse creations of his own Maker.

And there is, of course, the very wonderful story of the Stigmata. It was on Mount Alverno that he received a vision of the sufferings of Christ. So deeply did Francis meditate upon his Saviour's wounds that similar marks appeared on his own body.

What a wonderful man! A man who loved to laugh, and yet who was so close to his Lord as to share His very wounds. Most of all, he loved to love!

"Let all things their Creator bless, And worship Him in humbleness, O praise Him, Alleluia!"

40

"AT EVEN 'ERE THE SUN WAS SET"

A VERY lovely picture is painted by the words of this well-loved hymn, that of Jesus, the Great Healer, moved with compassion towards the sick and sad, healing them all. Undoubtedly, the author of this hymn had in mind such a picture when he wrote it.

The author was Canon Henry Twells, born at Ashted, near Birmingham, in 1823. He was for a time a master at St Andrew's School, Wells, Somerset.

This is by far the most popular hymn written by Canon Twells. At the time of his death he had authorised its inclusion in 157 hymnals throughout the English speaking world — a measure of its popularity.

I am glad to say that the Church is recovering its Ministry of Healing. For a long time, healing fell into disrepute because of its abuse and misuse by charlatans and rogues, so much so that good people kept clear of what they regarded as suspect.

But you cannot possibly read the Bible without appreciating the great importance Jesus placed upon healing the sick. And you are bound to notice something else — that Jesus never treated people just as bodies to be cured of this or that disease. Jesus saw them as *whole* persons. The division we make between body, mind and spirit is artificial and wrong.

Jesus never made that mistake. He came to set us free from whatever hurts or harms us in any part of our being. He instructed His Church to do two things: to preach the Gospel and heal the sick. In our Lord's mind the two things were inseparable.

So this world of today, in which you and I live is, I am

sure, the world where Christ heals. What I am saying is this: that the Gospel of Christ is so tremendous that it meets the needs of all people at every point. No one is left out. Our Lord's aim is nothing short of a world restored in which the healing of the nations is a natural consequence of His Presence and Power.

Canon Twells was absolutely right — Christ is here, waiting to heal us all:

"Once more 'tis eventide, and we
Oppressed with various ills, draw near.
What if Thy form we cannot see?
We know and feel that Thou art here".

Do you believe in praying for healing, either for yourself or for someone else? You should.

I can tell you of one answer to prayer. A little child lay dying in a Plymouth Hospital, the medical opinion being that she could not last through the night. In fact, to the trained eyes of the doctors it appeared that death had already set in. A young curate from St Andrew's came to see the child that evening. He felt a strong urge to spend the whole night in prayer for the child. This he did in the hospital Chapel. Next morning, to the utter astonishment of the staff, the child was still alive. She recovered and is now a university student. Only recently I met the Ward Sister at Weston-Super-Mare who told me that she has told this story to hundreds of student nurses ever since. The curate was my colleague, the Preb. John Parkinson.

Such a story could be multiplied many times! I have known many such answers to prayer in my own ministry.

In the last verse of this great hymn, we hear about the Touch of Christ — "Thy Touch hath still its ancient power." I believe that we can know the healing touch of Christ today, and that you and I can transmit that touch to others.

41

"HOW SWEET THE NAME OF JESUS SOUNDS"

IN THE Brontë Museum at Haworth in Yorkshire, among other little trinkets that belonged to Charlotte Brontë, are her scissors, blunted at the points because her gloomy father forbade pointed scissors in his house.

Those blunted scissors are a pathetic symbol of the blunted youth of the famous sisters — Charlotte, Emily and Anne, and their brother, Patrick Branwell. It is one of the great tragedies of English literature that such talented people should have had to live such grey, lonely, monotonous lives, hungering all the time for love and companionship.

They all died young — Patrick, at 31, Emily at 30, Anne at 29 and Charlotte, who survived them all, died at 39 just six months after her marriage which had brought her real happiness for the first time in her life.

All this happened in the Rectory at Haworth where their father was the incumbent for 41 years. He was an able, virtuous and conscientious parson, but he was totally unfitted to bring up his gifted, imaginative, sensitive children after their mother's death. He said he wished to make them "hardy and indifferent to eating and dress." They were not allowed to mix with other children. They were prisoners in their own home, and *all this in the name of religion.*

The Rev Patrick Brontë had got it wrong. Jesus did not mean His followers to live grey, monotonous lives, with long, unsmiling faces.

Jesus came to bring *Joy.* Yes, I know that Jesus is often described as the Man of Sorrows, but He was also the Radiant Christ with a gay, sparkling spirit like water that has been turned into wine.

The miracle of the Brontë family is that their genius was not suppressed by the heavy hand of a dull religion. Every word they ever wrote is eagerly snapped up and read. And in their writings you find a deep, passionate heart-hunger for love and sympathy.

"How sweet the Name of Jesus sounds" was written by John Newton, one-time infidel, whose own upbringing was not unlike that of the Brontës, but who came to see that Jesus Christ is the source of all joy and the fountain of all love. In an attempt to put into words his admiration for Jesus, Newton heaps title upon title — "Jesus my Prophet, Priest and King, my Lord, my Life, My Way, my End."

But who is this Jesus of whom John Newton sings? To some He is just a shadowy figure of history, very much a man of His own day, but hardly communicating with our modern age.

Pierre Teilhard de Chardin, a modern saint with a piercing vision, said that "Love is the most tremendous, the most universal, and the most mysterious of the cosmic forces."

Jesus Christ is Love personified. He did not just talk about it. He lived it. His kind of love always seeks the other person's good. His kind of love feeds the hungry. His kind of love brings joy. His kind of love succeeds where all else has failed. And nothing can destroy that kind of love. Death certainly cannot. It could not and it did not with Jesus.

And I am not surprised that John Newton, the sailor-preacher, wrote this hymn in praise of Jesus:

"Till then I would Thy love proclaim
With every fleeting breath;
And may the music of Thy Name
Refresh my soul in death."

42

"THE LORD'S MY SHEPHERD"

IT MAY not be realised just how great a revolution is taking place in hymn singing today. In most churches young people are encouraged to express their faith in modern language and modern ideas. In fact, if someone were to compile a new Ancient and Modern hymnbook for today, it would be very wide-ranging indeed. From the old favourite "Abide with me," to "God of concrete, God of Steel." From "Hark! the herald angels sing" to "Every star shall sing a carol."

When I remember that the twenty-third Psalm was first written at least three thousand years ago, I am amazed yet again at the power of the words of the Bible. When you come to think about it, words do not last all that time in our memory: perhaps a day or two, a week or two, even a year or two; but for words to last three thousand years! And likely to last as long as words themselves last! I find this amazing.

Think of how they came to be written: A teenager looks after his father's sheep in the fields at Bethlehem. As he learns the art of leading his sheep to good pasture and clear water, warding off the danger of marauding animals, and generally doing the work of a shepherd, he thinks "God is my shepherd, I shall not want, He leadeth me."

And when later young David, destined to become Israel's greatest King, wrote down his thoughts, he could not have known the extent to which those God-given words would comfort countless millions for the rest of time.

"The Lord's my shepherd" is a lovely hymn, especially when it is sung to "Crimond". The imagery throughout this Psalm is that of a shepherd — a shepherd remembers. So what was it in the words "Goodness and mercy shall follow me" that meant so much to David?

Picture the scene: the shepherd walks ahead of his sheep while the sheepdogs bring up the rear. The function of the dogs is to frighten off any wild animals that threaten the sheep, and, most of all, the dogs are there to keep the sheep together and prevent the lazy ones lagging too far behind the rest of the flock — you know what sheep are like! And if you have attended sheepdog trials you will know how highly skilled the sheepdog is.

Do you see what David is getting at in the twenty-third Psalm? "Goodness and Mercy" are the two dogs! You see, the Lord goes on ahead of us, and we are followed by goodness and mercy all the days of our lives.

It was after Francis Thompson had read these words that he wrote his greatest poem, "The Hound of Heaven".

The fact of the matter is, religion is not a pastime which we may or may not take up as we please. Religion deals with eternal realities which keep hunting us down an endless, hunting love no one ever really escapes. We can evade the challenge for a time, put off our response to its demands, but back it will come.

As a child, you may have played a kind of game called "Back to God", in which, no matter where you started, you found your way back to God. It was always so. It always will be. Jesus said: "I am the Good Shepherd. Follow me."

43

"BLESSED ASSURANCE JESUS IS MINE"

WHEN Independent Television ran a hymn-writing competition, something like eight thousand entries poured in, some of which were good, and a few very good indeed.

I have carried out a good deal of research in the field of hymns and their writers and I find that hymns get written for different reasons. In some instances, it is a matter of waiting for the inspiration to come. Again and again I have found that a hymn-writer has written only *one* hymn that stood the test of time.

But for some hymn-writers it has been a matter of sitting down and writing suitable words, crossing them out and writing more words until the thing comes right. Charles Wesley, Philip Doddridge and Isaac Watts all wrote hymns to order, sometimes for their own Sunday services, sometimes on themes suggested by other people.

The author of "Blessed Assurance, Jesus is mine" had her own way of writing hymns. Fanny Crosby became blind at the age of six, attended a School for the Blind in New York, and at 38 she married a blind musician. She lived to be 95. She wrote seven thousand hymns and sacred songs.

One of her close friends was a Mrs Knapp, whose husband was the founder of a Life Assurance Company. One day, Mrs Knapp played a melody on Fanny Crosby's piano and then said "What does the tune say?" At once the blind hymn-writer replied: "Blessed Assurance, Jesus is mine, O what a foretaste of glory divine!"

And so was born one of the most popular Gospel hymns of all time, so simple, so joyful that you cannot help singing and feeling it. Note that it is Blessed *Ass*urance" and not *Ins*urance". Mind you, some people do seem to think of religion as a kind of insurance policy! But Fanny Crosby had in mind the wonderful assurance of the presence and power of Jesus Christ.

For me, two things stand out in "Blessed Assurance" — Certainty and Serenity.

CERTAINTY — we live in an age that questions everything. Nothing is taken on trust, nothing is believed simply because it is said to be true. I do not deny the importance of the scientific method of critical inquiry, but the fact is that it has left us with precious little to be certain about, and so we lack the very quality Fanny Crosby writes about. I believe we have to be certain about a few things at least, and Fanny Crosby was certain about Jesus.

SERENITY — another quality sadly missing in most of us. The tempo of modern life, its stresses and strains drain us of nervous energy until we are left without a trace of real serenity of mind and spirit.

Serenity is the child of certainty. Fanny Crosby calls it "Blessed Assurance, Jesus is mine."

44

"O SACRED HEAD"

"O SACRED HEAD, once wounded" is among the world's oldest hymns. The original was written by a monk, Bernard of Clairvaux, 800 years ago. Five hundred years later, it was translated from Latin into German by Paul Gerhardt and published in 1656. It was later translated into English by James Waddell Alexander, and was first published in English in 1830. It has since gained universal acceptance and seems to have lost none of its original vitality by being translated from language to language. Johann Sebastian Bach greatly admired it and used it several times in his St Matthew Passion music.

Bernard of Clairvaux was a man who had cultivated the habit of meditation to a marked degree. Two stories illustrate this: On one occasion he paid a visit to the great monastery of La Grande Chartreuse in the mountainous country beyond Grenoble in France. Having heard so much about this man, his hosts were disappointed to find him riding such a splendid horse and sitting on so fine a saddle. It was, they felt, out of keeping with his strict monkish ways. After a while they plucked up the courage to mention it to Bernard who was surprised at their criticism. Although he had ridden many miles on it he hadn't noticed how fine the saddle was, and in any case the horse was not his but had been lent to him for the journey!

On another occasion it is said that when he was riding by the Lake of Geneva his companion asked him what he thought of the lake? "What lake?" asked Bernard!

This Christian saint so meditated upon the Death of Christ that it filled his entire being to the exclusion of all else. Bernard reflected on the grief and pain endured by the Saviour, the crown of thorns worn by the King of Kings, to such an extent that a legend says that when Bernard wrote this hymn, the image of Christ on the Cross bowed itself and embraced the saint with outstretched arms to betoken the acceptance of his devotion.

Listen to some of Bernard's marvellous words:

> "What language shall I borrow,
> To praise Thee, Heavenly friend,
> For this Thy dying sorrow,
> Thy pity without end?
> Lord make me Thine for ever,
> Nor let me faithless prove;
> O let me never, never
> Abuse such dying love."

There is a depth about this hymn that gives it a place among the immortals of hymnology. Some hymns are here today and gone tomorrow — they belong to a generation and pass with it. Not so with "O Sacred Head". As long as the human soul cries out for God this hymn will have a place in our sacred literature. It transcends all barriers of language and creed. It is a truly catholic hymn equally beloved of Christians of all denominations, a gift from God to the Universal Church.

It is when Christians contemplate the Death of Christ that they truly become one. All our man-made divisions fade into insignificance alongside the redemptive suffering of the Church's Sacred Head.

> "Be near me, Lord, when dying;
> O show Thyself to me."

45

HONEST DOUBT A HEALTHY
STATE OF MIND

IT IS surprising how a little we know about the twelve men whom Jesus chose to be His disciples. The Bible tells us very little about them in most cases, nothing at all in a few cases.

I wonder how much you think you know about Thomas? St. Thomas is the patron saint of builders since he is said to have taken the Gospel to India and built a church there with his own hands. We are given to understand from reliable traditions that he was martyred for his faith.

But if you were to ask almost anyone what he remembers most about Thomas it wouldn't be the church he built with his own hands in India or his martyrdom.

"Thomas?" people say, "ah yes, he was the doubter, the sceptic, the disciple who refused to believe that Jesus had risen from the dead." And so Thomas has come down through history with the label "Doubter" round his neck, and that is all that most people can tell you about him.

What a pity! There is far more to Thomas than his doubts.

There are three references to Thomas in the Bible, each providing us with a tiny window through which we can see the real man. They are all in St John's Gospel (chapters 11, 14 and 20). The first is about the time when Lazarus, a friend of our Lord's, was taken ill at his home in Bethany. Jesus decided to go to him. But the disciples protested — it was too dangerous for Him they said, and He might get killed. But it was Thomas who rallied the rest with the words: "Let us also go, that we might die with Him." A man of courage.

On another occasion, Jesus had been talking about His forthcoming death on the Cross. "You know where I am going," said Jesus to His disciples. As a matter of fact they didn't, but it is left to Thomas to ask the vital question: "Lord, we don't know where you are going, and how can we know the way?" And it was Thomas's question that brought from Jesus these immortal words, "I am the Way, I am the Truth, I am the Life."

The third incident is the one by which Thomas is most remembered. Jesus had risen from the dead and had appeared to His disciples in the Upper Room, but Thomas wasn't with them when Jesus came. When the others told him "We have seen the Lord!" his answer was "Except I see, I will not believe"— a very reasonable reply in the circumstances.

Eight days later Thomas was present when the Risen Christ came again. Jesus showed Thomas the wounds He had received on the Cross. Thomas saw and believed, confessing his belief with those memorable words, "My Lord and My God." Do you have doubts about the Christian faith? If you do there is nothing to be ashamed of — honest doubt is a healthy state of mind because it often leads to a discovery of the truth. Perhaps you are like Thomas and find spiritual truth hard to come by — if so, you aren't the only one. The thing to do with doubts is to bring them out into the open as Thomas did.

So "Doubting Thomas" built a church with his own hands, founded the Christian Church in India, and died a martyr for his faith.

Not bad for a doubter!

46

WHAT DO YOU DO IN A STORM?

A GREAT man of God was going through what we now call an emotional disturbance. Not many days before this came on he had seen his faith in God vindicated on a scale he had never imagined possible. But when we meet him he has taken to the hills and is living in a cave, convinced that people are out to kill him.

His troubled mind begins to play tricks on him. A gale-force wind blows up and for a moment he thinks he can hear the voice of God. But God is not in the wind.

Then an earthquake causes the loose rocks to crash down the mountainside, and again his fevered mind imagines that God is speaking to him. But God is not in the earthquake.

A fire breaks out, and because by this time his disturbed mind is ready to believe anything, even the crackling of the fire sounds to him like the voice of God. But God is not in the fire.

And then, when the wind, the earthquake and the fire had passed, God does speak to this man in "a still, small voice."

The man? Elijah, the Old Testament Prophet. Even though his mind was deeply troubled Elijah knew that God would come to him in his need. And He did. He always does.

As a minister it is my privilege to be with people in their deepest needs. I have watched them endure the storm of bereavement with a quiet strength born of God. I have seen ordinary men and women react to personal tragedy with a fortitude and a faith of which they would have thought themselves incapable. In the storm they have heard the "still, small voice" of God that alone makes sense of what has happened.

Most of us take shelter in a storm. At times there is little else to do. Yet storms come and we have to learn to live with them and through them.

One night I sat with a dying man. He had endured two years of mounting physical pain until during the last few days of his life it was almost unbearable. "Now," he said, "I think I know something of what Jesus meant when He cried on the Cross 'My God, My God, why hast Thou forsaken me?' "

That man was not gnashing his teeth at God. He might have done, for he was only forty-three. No, he was simply stating a fact of life — that often we get caught up in a storm. Over the years I have received hundreds of letters from viewers who have found themselves at the centre of a storm from which they could not break out.

By all means take shelter in a storm if it is available. There is, however, beauty in a storm. There is a strange majesty about a storm. The storm is a part of the beautiful natural world that God has made. And often the storm has much to teach us.

There is a scrap of conversation between two women in one of George Macdonald's books. One of them is saying "I wish I'd never been made!" To which the other replies, "My dear, you have not been made. You are being made and this is part of the Maker's process."

In one of Ibsen's plays, "Who taught thee to sing?" asks one character of another. And the answer comes back "God sent me sorrow."

There was a day in the life of Jesus when He heard His Father's voice so clearly. The crowd around Him said "It thunders!" Perhaps there was a thunderstorm on at the time! But Jesus said, "Father!"

We live in a world of many voices. It is like the Tower of Babel all over again — a great confusion of tongues. But if we are quiet enough, in the midst of the storm we shall hear the still, small voice of God.

Robert Browning wrote:

> "If I stoop into a dark tremendous sea of cloud,
> It is but for a time; I press God's lamp
> Close to my breast — its splendour, soon or late,
> Will pierce the gloom; I shall emerge one day."

When next you find yourself in the storm, remember that God is in it with you.

47

CHRIST AT CHRISTMAS

SO MUCH still to be done — cards to be sent, presents to be bought, food to be laid in, plus a hundred and one other jobs.

There always seems to be more money about before Christmas than ever before. Odd, isn't it, that this should be the case when so many people claim to be hard up and are therefore demanding higher salaries and wages. The signs of affluence are there for all to see.

But — and it is a big "but"— there are members of our society who really are poor by present-day standards, who won't be on a spending spree. I want to ask you to help such people.

I am not thinking primarily of giving money — that is often the easiest thing to do but not necessarily the right thing. There are many lonely people about and Christmas makes the lonely lonelier. As people filed out of my church one evening a lady said "Will you find me two lonely people we can invite to our home on Christmas Day?" Yes indeed! And what a lovely thing to do, so close to the heart of the Christ without whom there would be no Christmas.

Is this something you can do this Christmas? And remember, it isn't only the elderly who are lonely. Young folk also can be just as lonely and just as much in need of love at Christmas.

Christmas is the time for children, but there are children who will get a pretty thin time at Christmas unless someone does something about it.

I am sure you can think of cases of need right on your own doorstep. If you can't then think a bit harder and you will. Get in touch with the Social Services, your priest or minister, and see whether there isn't some way in which you can demonstrate the spirit of Christ.

It is far more blessed to give than to receive. In France and Germany they tell the story of the miracle of the apple. Hans was a very poor boy who more often than not was cold and hungry.

It was Christmas Eve and people were crowding the Cathedral at Strasbourg for the midnight Mass. As the people went in, Hans sheltered in a crevice of one of the large pillars at the entrance to the cathedral. A lady and her small daughter spotted him as he crouched there and gave him an apple as they went on into the warm building.

Hans did not eat the apple but kept it in his hand. Somehow he found himself inside the cathedral in a pew at the back. The service started. People stood up and sat down. They sang and they listened. Then Hans saw several fine gentlemen going up and down the rows of people, collecting money, He was terrified. He had no money to give. Perhaps the man would miss him. He didn't — they never do! And there was the collection plate right under his nose. Without thinking Hans put the apple on the plate. The man didn't bat an eyelid, but Hans was so ashamed; what would people think? And would he get into trouble?

He watched, mesmerised, as the man carried the plate to the front of the Cathedral, and there, standing out in the midst of the gold and silver coins, was his apple.

Then a marvellous thing happened. When the priest took the plate and raised it high in offering to God, the apple turned to gold and so became the best gift of all.

Do something for somebody at Christmas. Do it gladly, and do it for God. Who knows, your offering could be gold to somebody.

48

THE GLASTONBURY THORN

THE CHRISTIAN CHURCH has an emblem for everything, including the Nativity. To find it we have to go to Glastonbury and its famous legend.

The story goes that the man who buried Jesus, Joseph of Arimathea, was sent to bring the good news of the Gospel from Galilee to the Ancient Britons. It is said that when he came to Glastonbury he thrust his walking stick into the ground at Wirral Hill where it burst into blossom, buried the Holy Grail at Glastonbury Tor, and built a chapel of wattle and daub which later grew into the noble Norman Abbey which today stands magnificent in ruin.

If you visit Glastonbury at the right time of the year you will find the Glastonbury Thorn in bloom. It is a variety of hawthorn and is said to be the offspring of the one planted by Joseph of Arimathea long ago. The flowers are usually pink or red, and they come out in all their glory at Christmas. And so it is that the flower of the Glastonbury Thorn has become the emblem of the Nativity of Christ.

True, it is only a legend, but you will have difficulty in persuading the Glastonbury folk that it has no foundation in fact! As a matter of fact the Prophet Isaiah said this: "And there shall come forth a shoot out of the stock of Jesse, and a branch out of his roots shall bear fruit . . . He grew up before him as a tender plant, and as a root out of dry ground."

What Isaiah is here at pains to point out is that Jesus Christ would be a real person. Not a figment of pious imagination, but a man who would be bone of our bone, and flesh of our flesh.

Inevitably legends abound where Jesus is concerned —

legends about His birth, legends about His growing-up years, and legends about His life on earth generally. This was bound to happen.

But where Jesus is concerned we don't have to rely on legend. The facts about His life as they are recorded in the Bible are so stupendous that they make all the legends added together pale into insignificance. Here is God Himself, the Creator and Preserver of all mankind, being made in the likeness of a man. In Charles Wesley's words:

Our God contracted to a span,

Incomprehensibly made man."

You have heard me talk a great deal about the men who were the disciples of Jesus. They were not likely to be taken in by a figment of the imagination.They wanted more than a legend on which to build their lives. They lived and worked with Jesus for three years. They heard Him preach. They saw Him heal the sick and even raise the dead. And they saw the way in which Jesus Himself overcame death by rising from the dead. Their unanimous conclusion was: "Jesus Christ, born on Christmas Day, is both Lord and God."

The Glastonbury Thorn reminds us that the coming of Christ was the blossoming forth of a whole new way of life.

49

OPEN YOUR HANDS TO RECEIVE THE GIFT

NO MATTER how many pieces of music come and go, the "Messiah" goes on for ever. It is a work of sheer inspiration. Before he wrote this great oratorio, Handel tried his hand at opera and light music, without much success. Then, suddenly, like a man possessed, he began to write "Messiah". For twenty-three days, he worked almost without a break, filling nearly three hundred pages of manuscript with scarcely a correction. And the world will go on singing it as long as the human voice remains.

Think of some of the great Bible words Handel set to music: "For unto us a child is born, unto us a son is given: and the government shall be upon his shoulder; and his name shall be called Wonderful, Counsellor, the Mighty God, the Everlasting Father, the Prince of Peace."

I have learned something very important about Christmas — that when Jesus Christ came into the world, He came to give, not to receive. And yet see what happens. In almost every Nativity Play in church and school, everybody brings something to the Infant Christ. The Wise Men bring their gifts of gold and frankincense and myrrh, the shepherds bring their lambs, and indeed the whole world is depicted as bringing things to Christ as though He needed anything.

There is a lovely story written by Marjorie Proctor called "The Christmas Gift" in which she says that often our hands are so full that there is no room to receive the gifts which *He* wants to bring to *us* — the gifts of life and love and peace and joy. Only by emptying our hands, she says, can we receive the gifts Jesus has to offer.

I think there is a great truth in what Marjorie Proctor

says. Sometimes the thing we carry is so heavy, like the burden of anxiety. Jesus says "put it down, and take my rest." Or it may be the burden of fear. Again Jesus says: "Have faith, trust me. Let's go on together."

The fact of the matter is, our hands are too full. Too full of burdens. And what do we do? Why at Christmas we fill our hands still fuller and come to the Manger Crib offering gifts galore when we ought instead to be taking the gifts He came to bring.

I ask you to open your hands, your heart, your mind, your life, and take the gift of Jesus Christ right in. In the service of Holy Communion, the heart of the matter comes when the communicants *take* the bread and the wine — what a tragedy it would be if their hands were too full to receive the symbols of redeeming love!

"Unto us a Son is given."

50

JOY TO THE WORLD

WHEN JESUS was born, Joy came to the world. The angels sang "Glory to God in the highest! Peace on earth to men of goodwill!" What a joyful sound that must have been.

We talk too much of duty and sacrifice and discipline — these are dull and colourless words. I want to talk about the JOY of being a Christian. Joy is not a weak word. It is not resignation wearing a pale smile. It is strong and deep and effervescent. Did you know that Christians are told to 'rejoice' no fewer than seventy times in the New Testament? Read the story of the beginnings of the Christian Church and you will see joy written across the faces of the first Christians. At Pentecost their joy bubbled over to such an extent that many supposed them to be drunk — that was the only explanation the world could put upon their behaviour!

The stiff, the staid and the starchy have always regarded Christian joy as slightly vulgar. A man once said to me "show me a church where the people laugh and I will go to it." Are there really so few such churches? The fact remains, wherever there has been a genuine turning to religion, the experience has expressed itself in a joy that bubbles over.

The early Franciscans had it. So had the early Methodists and Salvationists. There is a lovely story told about a Salvation Army drummer who was asked not to hit his drum quite so hard — "Lor' bless you," he replied, "since I've been converted, I'm so happy, I could burst the blooming drum!"

Billy Bray, Cornwall's own evangelist, used to say that when he walked along the Cornish lanes, even the trees clapped their hands because "the King's son was passing by." And that if he were to be put in a beer-barrel, he would shout "Praise the Lord!" through the bung-hole! So why is it that when some of us are observed going into church we look as if we are going to the dentist's, and when we come out, as if we have been!

What an impact Jesus must have made on people. No other religious leader in history had spoken of joy the way Jesus did. Life, He said, was more like a wedding than a funeral. "I have spoken thus to you," He said, "so that MY JOY may be in you, and your joy complete."

When I was the Superintendent of the Edinburgh Methodist Mission, the old men there still talked of a young minister who had come to them fifty years before. Dr. George Jackson, they told me, "brought us the Gospel of Joy."

WHAT IS JOY?

Have you seen a copse of bluebells lifting their tiny faces to the morning sun through a rainbow mist? This is joy.

Have you seen a dolphin leaping high out of the sparkling sea, or little wavelets gently caressing the rocks on a calm summer's day? This is joy.

Have you heard a lark singing on the topmost branch of a tree, and have you seen it spreading its wings and flying upwards into a deep blue sky? This is joy.

Have you seen the love on the face of a dear one coming forward, arms outstretched, to greet you? This is joy.

To have known all these beautiful things, and more, is to know the flights of the soul to God, and His love.

To know the Christ in every atom of the Cosmos. This is pure joy. God's own gift of joy for you.

As we stand between Christmas and New Year, let us open our hearts to receive the One who is the source of all our joys — "Jesu, Joy of Man's desiring."

Will you pray with me?

"O Thou who art the very spirit of joy, grant us the reality of inward happiness, the serenity that comes from living close to Thee. At this time of new beginnings, daily renew in us the sense of Joy. Let Thy eternal spirit dwell in our hearts so that, bearing about with us the infection of a radiant joy, we may dwell in the secret place, giving thanks to Thee always, through Jesus Christ, our Joy and our Redeemer. Amen."